The Decline and Fall
of Hemispheric Specialization

The Decline and Fall
of Hemispheric Specialization

Robert Efron
Professor of Neurology
School of Medicine
University of California at Davis
and
Associate Chief of Staff for Research & Development
Veterans Administration Medical Center
Martinez, CA

LEA LAWRENCE ERLBAUM ASSOCIATES, PUBLISHERS
1990   Hillsdale, New Jersey   Hove and London

Lawrence Erlbaum Associates, Inc., Publishers
365 Broadway
Hillsdale, New Jersey 07642

Library of Congress Cataloging-in-Publication Data

Efron, Robert
    The decline and fall of hemispheric specialization / by Robert
Efron.
       p.   cm.
    Lectures delivered at the MacEachran lectures for 1989 at the
University of Alberta on Oct. 16–18, 1989.
    Includes bibliographical references.
    ISBN 0-8058-0716-0
    1. Cerebral dominance. 2. Cognitive science. I. Title.
    [DNLM: 1. Dominance, Cerebral. WL 335 E27d]
    QP385.5.E36 1990
    612.8'25--dc20
    DNLM/DLC
    for Library of Congress   90-2715
                                       CIP

Printed in the United States of America
10 9 8 7 6 5 4 3 2

To Barbara,
Without whom none of it would
have been as much fun.

Contents

Preface

When invited to present the MacEachran lectures for 1989 at the University of Alberta, I was asked to speak on the subject of hemispheric differences in human cognitive activity. Although I felt most honored to be included among the distinguished list of previous MacEachran lecturers, my initial response was to decline. My principal reason was that for many years I have had profound doubts about the validity of too many of the fundamental assumptions and claims of this discipline. With this level of skepticism, I felt that I should not be the first MacEachran lecturer to provide an overview of this field. My hesitation was finally overcome when Professor Lechelt, who tendered the invitation, insisted that healthy criticism is essential in science and that in this discipline, more than most, it was sorely needed. I succumbed, but with the provision that I would not present a review of the extensive literature of the subject but a personal overview of a *few* of the central problems I had identified.

While preparing the three lectures I found that the assignment was more difficult than I had anticipated, not only because of the *enormity* of the literature I was reviewing but the *variety* of epistemological, conceptual, and methodological issues that needed to be addressed. Obviously, I had to be highly selective. This slender volume thus represents what I believe to be the most significant issues — it is one man's point of view. To ensure as balanced an overview as possible, I make reference to many books, review articles, and research reports that present opposing positions. Nevertheless, the conclusions expressed here, occasionally less diplomatically than is usual in science, will be rejected by many readers. For them, this book will be perceived as a *minority* report. On the other hand, these conclusions may

x

reflect the views of a "silent majority" of cognitive neuroscientists who simply have not considered it worth the effort to point out that "the emperor has no clothes."

I have retained as much as possible of the informal lecture format in the book. Having written too many research papers in the desiccated style required by scientific journals, I seized this opportunity to write as I prefer. These three chapters contain all the material that was presented orally in the lectures. Additional material has been included in the published version without altering the informal style of the oral presentation. The Mac-Eachran lectures were given on October 16th, 17th, and 18th in 1989.

Acknowledgments

In the preparation of these lectures, I have received assistance from many individuals. Three of them have special status: My wife, Barbara, read every lecture and chapter innumerable times and was instrumental in seeing that I was communicating my views in as comprehensible a fashion as possible. She was also my collaborator in the experiments performed on the patient with visual agnosia described in Chapter 1. The second "special" person is Bill Yund who has been a friend and scientific collaborator since 1974. When I use the word "we" in the text, it is not the "imperial" mode of expression but means Bill and me. We have worked together every day on so many projects in the past 15 years that neither of us is ever certain who was responsible for which idea (the good ones or the bad ones). Because we could never make this distinction, we adopted the policy of alternating senior authorship of all joint papers. Finally, I am indebted to Davis Howes who carefully reviewed the manuscript and made many valuable suggestions that were incorporated in the final text. None of these individuals, of course, is in any way responsible for my choice of topics, style, or emphasis, or for any factual errors.

Last, but surely not least, I would like to take this opporunity to acknowledge the U.S. Veterans Administration, which has provided uninterrupted financial support for my research since 1960. Without this concrete expression of confidence, I would not have performed any of the experiments described here nor had the time or resources to prepare this book.

John M. MacEachran
Memorial Lecture Series

The Department of Psychology at the University of Alberta inaugurated the MacEachran Memorial Lecture Series in 1975 in honor of the late Professor John M. MacEachran. Professor MacEachran was born in Ontario in 1877 and received a Ph.D. in Philosophy from Queen's University in 1905. In 1906 he left for Germany to begin more formal study in psychology, first spending just less than a year in Berlin with Stumpf, and then moving to Leipzig, where he completed a second Ph.D. in 1908 with Wundt as his supervisor. During this period he also spent time in Paris studying under Durkheim and Henri Bergson. With these impressive qualifications the University of Alberta was particularly fortunate in attracting him to its faculty in 1909.

Professor MacEachran's impact has been signficant at the university, provincial, and national levels. At the University of Alberta he offered the first courses in psychology and subsequently served as Head of the Department of Philosophy and Psychology and Provost of the University until his retirement in 1945. It was largely owing to his activities and example that several areas of academic study were established on a firm and enduring basis. In addition to playing a major role in establishing the Faculties of Medicine, Education and Law in this Province, Professor MacEachran was also instrumental in the formative stages of the Mental Health Movement in Alberta. At a national level, he was one of the founders of the Canadian Psychological Association and also became its first Honorary President in 1939. John M. MacEachran was indeed one of the pioneers in the development of psychology in Canada.

Perhaps the most significant aspect of the MacEachran Memorial Lecture

Series has been the continuing agreement that the Department of Psychology at the University of Alberta has with Lawrence Erlbaum Associates, Publishers, Inc., for the publication of each lecture series. The following is a list of the Invited Speakers and the titles of their published lectures:

1975 Frank A. Geldard (Princeton University)
    "Sensory Saltation: Metastability in the Perceptual World"

1976 Benton J. Underwood (Northwestern University)
    "Temporal Codes for Memories: Issues and Problems"

1977 David Elkind (Rochester University)
    "The Child's Reality: Three Developmental Themes"

1978 Harold Kelley (University of California at Los Angeles)
    "Personal Relationships: Their Structures and Processes"

1979 Robert Rescorla (Yale University)
    "Pavlovian Second-Order Conditioning:
    Studies in Associative Learning"

1980 Mortimer Mishkin (NIMH-Bethesda)
    "Cognitive Circuits" (*unpublished*)

1981 James Greeno (University of Pittsburgh)
    "Current Cognitive Theory in Problem Solving" (*unpublished*)

1982 William Uttal (University of Michigan)
    "Visual Form Detection in 3-Dimensional Space"

1983 Jean Mandler (University of California at San Diego)
    "Stories, Scripts, and Scenes: Aspects of Schema Theory"

1984 George Collier and Carolyn Rovee-Collier (Rutgers University)
    "Learning and Motivation: Function and
    Mechanism" (*unpublished*)

1985 Alice Eagly (Purdue University)
    "Sex Differences in Social Behavior:
    A Social-Role Interpretation"

1986 Karl Pribram (Stanford University)
    "Brain and Perception:
    Holonomy and Structure in Figural Processing" (*in press*)

1987 Abram Amsel (University of Texas at Austin)
    "Behaviorism, Neobehaviorism, and Cognitivism in
    Learning Theory: Historical and Contemporary Perspectives"

1988   Robert S. Siegler and Eric Jenkins (Carnegie-Mellon University)
"How Children Discover New Strategies"

1989   Robert Efron (University of California at Davis & Veterans
Administration Medical Center)
"The Decline and Fall of Hemispheric Specialization"

Eugene C. Lechelt, Coordinator
MacEachran Memorial Lecture Series

Sponsored by The Department of Psychology, The University of Alberta with the support of The Alberta Heritage Foundation for Medical Research in memory of John M. MacEachran, pioneer in Canadian psychology.

1

The Decline of Hemispheric Specialization

INTRODUCTION

Every reader of this book — indeed everyone who reads a daily newspaper — has heard that the left hemisphere is specialized for language, mathematics, detailed analysis, logical thought, temporal and sequential analysis, and serial processing of sensory information. You also have heard that the right hemisphere is specialized for emotional expression, intuition, the recognition of faces and the emotions expressed in faces, artistic achievement, attention, recognition of musical passages and other musical aptitudes, visual-spatial analysis, and parallel processing of sensory information.

Over the past 30 years a number of investigators have periodically attempted to reduce the multiple specializations of each hemisphere to a single, more encompassing, function. Of course, since there are only two hemispheres, the two global functions must necessarily be expressed in a dichotomous fashion. Thus you have also heard that the left hemisphere is specialized for "verbal" functions whereas the right hemisphere is specialized for "non-verbal" ones; or that the left hemisphere is specialized for "linguistic" functions and the right for "visual-spatial" functions; or that the left hemisphere is specialized for detailed, "analytic" functions, whereas the right hemisphere provides us with a big picture of the world, as it is specialized for "holistic" functions; or that the left hemisphere is specialized for "propositional" functions, whereas the right hemisphere is specialized for "appositional" functions. Although none of these dichotomies has successfully integrated the wide variety of diverse functions attributed to each hemisphere, and almost no one today accepts them as valid

1

generalizations, they nevertheless paved the way for the concept that there are left- and right-hemisphere "cognitive styles" or personality types — terms that, as you might expect, are commonly used either humorously or pejoratively, as illustrated in Fig. 1.

These global abstractions have been extended far beyond the realm of neuropsychology itself, and have spawned imaginative new disciplines called "neuropolitics," "neuroanthropology," and "neurosociology" (Ten Houten, 1985). These disciplines purport to account for the differences between Western and Oriental philosophies, our political ideologies, as well as the communication gap between generations, by the degrees to which our two hemispheres come to differ in their panoply of talents, styles or modes of cognition as a consequence of our education, social class (in the sense used by Karl Marx), urbanization, culture, and native language. The *political* implications of the concept of hemispheric specialization are now considered to be so self-evident that it has been seriously argued in some quarters that our European-based educational system, with its heavy emphasis on teaching the young to read, write, and do arithmetic, is in blatant violation of the constitutional rights of the right hemisphere to an equal education!

Some of these claims involving the differential specialization of the two hemispheres have been dismissed by serious scholars as unwarranted overgeneralizations from the known facts by "academic hucksters" or "non-professionals." These same scholars also have acknowledged that the field of what has now come to be called "laterality research" has been characterized by a disproportionately large number of contradictions and failures

"EVERY ONCE IN A WHILE MY
RIGHT BRAIN THROWS SOMETHING IN."

FIGURE 1. Copyright 1984 by Sidney Harris, originally published in *American Scientist* magazine. Reproduced by permission of Sidney Harris.

to replicate the experimental results of others. At least one of them has voiced his suspicion that there has been a strong tendency for selective publication of results that are consistent with the prevailing theoretical Zeitgeist and thus "interesting," with a parallel tendency to ignore work that does not fit or support the prevailing views (Bertelson, 1982).

These problems of laterality research have been so thoroughly discussed by others, most notably Bryden (1982), Bertelson (1982), Beaumont (1982), Corballis (1983), and the open peer commentaries on the paper by Bradshaw and Nettleton (1981), that I will not attempt to document them once again. Instead, my purpose in this chapter is to discuss some of the deeper theoretical and epistemological problems entailed by the concept of hemispheric specialization for cognitive functions that some of these books, review articles, and book chapters have alluded to but not addressed adequately. I provide concrete examples to illustrate how these issues affect the way research findings are interpreted and why the failure to understand the epistemological problems of the field has led to the misguided views about hemispheric specialization that I have just described. In Chapter 2 I go one step further and show how these unresolved problems have led the field of laterality research into a state of total scientific collapse. Chapter 3 offers a viable solution.

THE MEANING OF "SPECIALIZATION"

Before we can even begin to consider the issues in this complex area, it is first necessary to distinguish between the uses of the term "specialization" by neurophysiologists and by neuropsychologists. There is absolutely no doubt that various cells in the nervous system have markedly different properties: The rods and cones of the retina are exquisitely sensitive to light, the hair cells in the cochlea to mechanical displacement, cells in the medulla to minute changes in carbon dioxide concentration, and cells in the striate cortex that respond with high rates of discharge to one orientation of a pattern but not to another. Even at subcellular levels, the membrane responses to specific neurotransmitters, for example, are highly selective. Although such uniquely specific responses of single cells and their components are usually referred to as "selectivity" by neurophysiologists, it is neither an abuse of language nor does it create any ambiguity of meaning to say that they are "specialized" in their *response characteristics* in precisely definable ways.

It is also the case that cells with certain types of selective responses are not distributed randomly within the brain, but highly concentrated in certain areas. Thus there are reasonably well-defined areas containing cells that have specific responses to visual, auditory, olfactory, or tactile stimuli, and these areas are appropriately referred to as visual, auditory, olfactory, or tactile "centers." There are also motor centers that, if stimulated electrically, give rise to specific, definable muscular contractions, for example, the frontal eye fields, which play an important role in eye movement control. However, the cells within such a center, say, the visual center in the lateral geniculate nucleus of the thalamus or the one in the striate cortex, are aggregates of interconnected cells having *different* types of selective responses. Although it is not difficult to define in what way a *single neurone* is "specialized," it is not a trivial task to define the specialized function of such a "center," whether it be a sensory or motor one. It is when we attempt to deal with very large numbers of interconnected neurones, each having different selectivities, that the concept of "specialization" of function becomes exceedingly difficult to apply. For example, after more than 30 years of intensive research on single neurones in the striate cortex, it is clear that its individual cells have many different types of selective responses, but it still is not possible to formulate a single abstraction that adequately defines the principal function(s) of this critically important and anatomically well-demarcated region of the cerebral cortex — despite the fact that monkeys and men are essentially blind if this area is destroyed bilaterally. Indeed, it would be fair to say that most visual neurophysiologists would consider it somewhat silly, given our present knowledge, even to attempt such an abstraction. If pushed, they might say that it is at the striate cortex that the radial symmetry of the center- surround discharge pattern of single neurones of the lateral geniculate is changed to a bilaterally symmetrical discharge pattern, and that this may indicate the *first* step in the Fourier analysis by which a two-dimensional spatial frequency map is created.

In contrast, when neuropsychologists use the term "specialization" they mean something quite different from the neurophysiological concept of "selective response." They mean that a particular region of the brain is critically responsible for the performance of a specific cognitive *function* or a small group of closely related cognitive sub-functions. It should be emphasized that the root concepts and vocabularies of neurophysiology and neuropsychology do not overlap, except with respect to anatomical issues. This is not surprising since one discipline deals with *brain* functions whereas the other deals with *mental* functions. Indeed, until such time as the mind body dichotomy is resolved, these vocabularies will continue to differ.

The field of neuropsychology, however, has a unique problem that is not shared by the two disciplines to which it is conceptually related. Cognitive psychologists do not have to relate their findings to any neuroanatomical or neurophysiological data. For them the brain can be considered merely a "black box." Neuropsychologists, however, are not so fortunate: The implicit mandate for their field is to relate mental phenomena to the internal structure and function of that black box. Given this mandate, their conceptualizations, vocabulary, and methodology will inevitably be less "pure" epistemologically, and thus more subject to criticism, than those of neurophysiology or cognitive psychology. This burden should make them *more* careful when they define their terms, state their inferences, and evaluate their evidence. Unfortunately, such epistemological fastidiousness is rarely exhibited.

INFERRING FUNCTION FROM BEHAVIORAL DEFICITS

Having said that neuropsychology uses the term "specialization" to mean that a particular region of the brain is critically responsible for the performance of a specific cognitive function, I now want to discuss the inferential procedures that are used to make such a claim. Historically, the primary method used to determine the function of some region of the nervous system has been to see what deficit results if that area is damaged by disease (or by an overly zealous neurosurgeon). Although this approach has generated a vast and scientifically exciting body of information, it is not as easy as you might imagine to infer the *function* of the tissue that has been physically or biochemically damaged from the observable *deficit*.

As this difficulty is central to any evaluation of the claims for hemispheric specializations with which I began this chapter, I will illustrate the problem with two examples. The first relates to a characteristic behavioral deficit that is seen when the cerebellum is damaged. In such cases, when the patient is asked to touch an object with his finger tip he will reach out in the appropriate direction but will alternately over- and under-shoot the target. This readily observable behavioral deficit has been called "dysmetria." Many neurologists had concluded that one of the *functions* of the cerebellum is to *inhibit* this over- and under-shooting. Over 40 years ago, in a discussion of dysmetria, F.M.R. Walshe rejected the inference that the cerebellum has an inhibitory "braking" function, and as part of a longer argument used the following analogy (Walshe, 1947): Imagine, he said, an automobile transmission system, crudely illustrated in Fig. 2, in which one tooth of a gear has been knocked off, by the kind of stroke that affects all of our cars from time to time. Because the loss of this one tooth does not render the gear-train totally inoperative, the only striking behavioral deficit of which we are aware is a "thunk" that is heard on every revolution of the drive shaft when it is turned slowly, and a vibration at higher speeds. Now what is the function of this missing tooth? What did it do *before* it was knocked off? To someone who knows as little about mechanical systems as we know about cerebral function, an apparently plausible answer is that the *function* of the missing gear tooth is to prevent or inhibit the "thunk" and

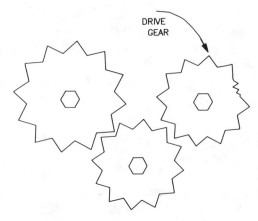

FIGURE 2. Inferring the function of the missing gear tooth on the drive shaft from the "thunk" heard on each revolution. Example of F.M.R. Walshe (1947). See text for discussion.

vibration. Further, if the tooth is welded back on, and the symptoms disappear, the hypothesis regarding its inhibitory function appears to be supported. The actual function of the gear teeth — to transmit power from the drive to the driven shaft — has been missed entirely!

The point of Walshe's clever example is to warn us that if we define the *function* of a region of the brain in terms of the *symptom* that results if it is damaged, then it is almost inevitable that we will *misidentify* its actual function. Thus, if a stroke in some area of the brain results in the inability to tie one's shoe laces, while the performance of all other bimanual tasks, such as typing and cutting steak at the dinner table, are intact, we inevitably would be led to the almost certainly erroneous conclusion that the *function* of the tissue prior to the damage was to tie shoe laces, that it is "specialized" for this function.

Let us now consider the behavioral deficit in another machine, one appreciably more complicated than Walshe's gear-train, but vastly less complicated even than the brain of a bird. I refer now to my desk top computer. Imagine that, while I am working happily on my computer adding a set of numbers from a file and displaying the sum on the screen, a cosmic ray particle strikes one particular chip in the computer and damages it. I suddenly notice that some, but not all, of my additions are producing absolutely bizarre results. As a neurologist, I suspect that my computer has developed what is known in the trade as an acalculia, a specific deficit in performing simple arithmetic functions seen in some patients with strokes. Further diagnostic tests reveal that major errors occur not only in addition, but subtraction, multiplication, and *every* other numeric operation, providing additional evidence that the computer has developed an acalculia. When the repairman replaces the defective chip, moreover, the acalculia disappears, "converging evidence" supporting my inference that this particular chip is "specialized" for mathematical functions.

Now what actually has happened is that one of the functions of the chip is to convert a few bit patterns corresponding to decimal digits into the proper numerical characters, and that when damaged this conversion fails — every time a bit pattern representing a 1 is sent to the chip, the defective chip converts it to a 9 which is then displayed on the screen. My computer's behavioral deficit was only that the numerical result *as displayed on the screen* was incorrect. Had I known more about computers, I could have tested this hypothesis directly by sending the numbers to be printed on a piece of paper, rather than on the screen. Since computer printers contain a chip having a similar function, and the one in the printer was *not* hit by the cosmic particle, all digits would have been printed correctly on the paper, thus demonstrating that the computer had never suffered from an acalculia at all. Finally, without having performed a very large number of diagnostic tests on the computer, I would never know what other functions of the chip had been damaged.

I would maintain, and I'm sure you will agree, that by disregarding Walshe's warning not to confuse the symptom with the function I had made an egregious error in concluding that the chip was "specialized" to perform calculations, or that its function was to calculate. I also would maintain that it is our exceedingly primitive understanding of the unimaginably complex neural mechanisms underlying language, calculation, and other cognitive functions that predisposes us to confuse the observed behavioral deficit, the symptom, with the actual function or functions of that tissue *prior* to the damage.

LOCALIZATION VERSUS SPECIALIZATION

My purpose in using the gear-train and computer analogies is to focus attention on two closely related concepts that, more than any others, have been the source of epistemological chaos in the field of neuropsychology — the concepts of *localization and specialization* of function. I have already pointed out that visual neurophysiologists still are unable to define the function of the striate cortex, despite the fact that primates become essentially blind if this cortical area is damaged bilaterally. Similarly, we cannot yet define the functions of the left fronto-temporal lobe despite the fact that in more that 95% of human beings profound disturbances of language occur if this area is damaged. But what is added to our understanding of the actual functions of these two areas if this knowledge is restated by saying that one is "specialized for vision," and that the other is "specialized for language"? Absolutely nothing.

Most neuropsychologists insist that they use this word *only* as a *shorthand expression* to refer to these correlations between lesion site and symptom. Although this may have been the original intention, even a cursory review of the literature supports my contention that this is no longer the case. Over time they have come to believe that a function called vision is "located" in the striate cortex, when it is no more "located" there than in the retina, optic nerve, or parastriate cortex, and that the function called language is "located" in the left fronto-temporal area. Expressed in another way, this scientifically empty restatement of the facts has predisposed them to forget that the striate cortex and left fronto-temporal cortex are only *components* of anatomically extensive visual and linguistic *systems*.

Recent research using PET and SPECT brain imaging provides compelling evidence that many different areas of the brain in *both* hemispheres become metabolically active when we engage in a specific cognitive activity. These maps, now in pseudo-Technicolor, reveal that neural circuits supporting a cognitive function are located in anatomically disparate regions and that the *same* areas may become active in two distinctly different cognitive activities, for example, actually moving your hand and *imagining* that you are moving your hand. This *physiological* evidence underscores my point: that use of the term "specialization of function" has predisposed neuropsychologists to believe that a specific cognitive function is performed "in" a specific cerebral area, which is "specialized" for that cognitive activity, rather than by an anatomically extensive system involving both hemispheres.

At a deeper level, however, when the term specialization of function is used as a short-hand way of referring to a *correlation* between the site of a lesion and some cognitive symptom, the short-hand user is predisposed to confuse a correlation with an explanation or hypothesis. A correlation is testable by repeating, with more patients, the incidence of various cognitive deficits with lesions at different brain sites. Regardless of the strength, and the reproducibility of the correlation, it does not explain *why* this relationship is observed, or permit any *prediction* outside of itself.

A correlation is *not* a hypothesis: In the development of a science, a correlation is a *first* step, albeit a necessary one, which must, if it is to go anywhere, be followed up by a tentative explanation—the hypothesis itself—whose predictions are then tested by well-designed experiments. If this procedure is not followed, as is often the case among neuropsychologists, it leads to circular and misleading statements such as, "The patient cannot speak *because* the center for speech production has been damaged, but he can understand speech *because* the center for speech comprehension is intact." It is *circular* since it refers to no further information than that contained in the initial clinical-pathological correlation, and it is *misleading* since it predisposes the speaker, as well as the unwary listener, to believe that an explanation has been offered when it hasn't.

Another statement, found in many articles and books, is even more misleading: "It is unarguable that the left hemisphere is specialized for language." This covertly implies that some scholars dispute the validity of the clinical-pathological correlation, or are unaware of it — when neither is the case — and leaves the unwary reader with the distinct impression that any objections to this proposition could only come from an ignoramus who still believes that the earth is flat! When I object to such misleading formulations, most neuropsychologists look at me incredulously and ask, "Are you saying that the left hemisphere is *not* specialized for language?" or "On what grounds do you reject this hypothesis?", failing to remember that their concept of specialization has the status of an observed correlation between the symptom and a lesion location but is not a *refutable* scientific hypothesis concerning the actual function of the damaged tissue. It is not refutable, of course, since the function has been *defined* in terms of the symptom.

What *is* indisputable is that the *strongest* correlation between the localization of the brain lesion and a cognitive dysfunction is for language functions: More than 95% of the population will develop one or another type of language disturbance, an aphasia, following a left fronto-temporal stroke. The existence of this correlation undoubtedly indicates that this brain region contains neural circuits that support language functions, but it does not necessarily mean that the function called "language" is performed by these circuits. It is more likely that these circuits perform a variety of functions, some of which are *required* for normal language function. This is precisely the point that Walshe made with his gear-train analogy: Don't confuse the function with the symptom.

Despite the existence of this strong correlation between the symptoms of aphasia and lesions in the left fronto-temporal region, it has been known for over 100 years that even with large lesions extending well beyond the area of the so-called language centers in the left fronto-temporal area, some speech remains. A patient with such a large lesion may be incapable of verbally communicating any simple wish or idea but, perhaps in frustration or despair, will sometimes curse or utter other expletives with perfect articulation and may even sing common songs, *using words*, with some degree of proficiency.

Such observations led neurologists in the late 19th century to suspect that this "residual" language is accomplished by speech centers in mirror-image locations within the *right* hemisphere and that recovery from aphasia might be due to the right-sided areas "taking over" language functions that could no longer be performed by the damaged tissue on the left side. This suspicion was supported by the fact that *recovered* aphasics who subsequently had a stroke in their *right* hemisphere developed a profound and *lasting* aphasia. More recent evidence indicates that with careful testing of right- handed patients with right hemisphere lesions subtle language disturbances can be detected, and that in split-brain subjects whose fronto-temporal areas in both hemispheres are undamaged, the right hemisphere, like a 2-year old, appears to "understand" vastly more speech than it can express (Ardila, 1984; Zaidel, 1985).

The right hemisphere's apparent capacity to understand spoken language will be discussed again in Chapter 2 in the context of dichotic listening experiments. For the moment, however, I call your attention to the curious fact that those who assert that it is indisputable that the left hemisphere is "specialized for language" usually are aware that damage to the mirror-image regions of the right hemisphere often result in disturbances of the prosodic and intonational aspects of spoken language (Ross, 1981; Ross & Mesulam, 1979). However, they rarely say that the right hemisphere is "also specialized for language, but less so or differently": They seem more comfortable in using the phrase "right-hemisphere speech," and dropping the term specialization in this case. These same neuropsychologists also know that aphasia occurs following lesions in the thalamus, a subcortical area far removed from the so-called speech centers in *either* hemisphere (Damasio & Damasio, 1989; Ojemann, Fedio, & Van Buren, 1968; Ojemann & Ward, 1971; and *BRAIN AND LANGUAGE*, 1975, *2*, 1–120, for a series of review articles.). To be consistent, they should describe the thalamus as "specialized for language," but I have *never* heard this formulation used, and when I use it to point out their logical inconsistency, a bewildered expression crosses their faces!

Finally, there are interesting patients who have lost their hearing before speech developed and who learned to communicate by signing. A recent report of a left-hemisphere stroke in one such patient (Chiarello, Knight, & Mandel, 1982) describes the typical manifestations of aphasia but in sign language. However, the cerebral damage was *not* in the area usually considered to be a language area, the region near the auditory cortex, but rather, in a region where sensory information from the hands reaches the cortex. Thus, for this individual, who had learned to use a manual means of communication, neural circuits supporting linguistic functions developed in somesthetic cortex. To be consistent, one should then say that the somesthetic cortex is "specialized for language."

Such logical consistency has not been followed, I suspect, because it would make it even more evident that the many different, and at present unidentified, sub-functions required for efficient language comprehension or production are not "located" in one or two cortical areas but are supported by an anatomically extensive *system*, a point of view that runs counter to the neuropsychologist's agenda but which is nevertheless *visible* in PET and SPECT images. In using the word "agenda," I do not mean to imply any conspiracy, but rather to emphasize that the original role of the neuropsychologist, when arteriograms or CAT and MRI scans did not exist, was to assist the neurologist in localizing the patient's *lesion* using psychological measures. It is easy to understand that this historical role led to the misconception, unfortunately still prevalent, that they were localizing the defective cognitive *function*.

In sum, although there is overwhelming evidence that many important neural circuits supporting language functions are indeed located in the left fronto-temporal area, it is evident that neural circuits are present and/or can be developed in a number of *other* cerebral areas that also support these functions. By now you must have noticed that I have repeatedly used the phrase "neural circuits that *support*" a function and have abjured the phrase "neural circuits that are *specialized*" for a function. I will continue to use this neurophysiologist's vocabulary for three reasons: (1) It does not confuse the symptom with the yet-to-be-discovered function; (2) It does not convey any hidden and misleading implications with respect to the *location* of a cognitive function; and (3) It does not confuse a correlation with an explanation.

REDUCTION OF MULTIPLE BEHAVIORAL DEFICITS
TO ONE COGNITIVE DEFICIT

My discussion so far has been focused exclusively on the problems entailed in inferring the function of a cerebral area from the behavioral deficit observed when that region is damaged. I turn now to a related, and even more difficult, problem of inference. In virtually all cases of brain damage, even from a relatively circumscribed lesion, there are a number of different behavioral deficits that become evident as the investigator tests the patient with various tasks. The issue is how to decide whether there are multiple, unrelated, and essentially *different* cognitive functions that have been impaired simultaneously, or a *single* impaired cognitive function that underlies or accounts for all the behavioral deficits. I will illustrate this issue in a patient with a rather dramatic set of behavioral deficits that resulted from diffuse, bilateral brain damage (Efron, 1969). The nature of this inferential process, however, is identical whether the patient's lesion is in one hemisphere only or in both, or whether it is a focal or diffuse lesion.

A young soldier slept overnight in a room with a defective space heater and suffered a massive overdose of carbon monoxide. When found in the morning, he was comatose and remained in a deep coma for some days because of the widespread neuronal damage throughout his brain. As he slowly regained his ability to speak and understand, he appeared to be blind. Except for a normal reflex contraction of his pupils to light, he seemed to have no useful vision at all. He lay in bed with his eyes roving the visual scene in an apparently random fashion. On more careful examination several days later, however, it was evident that he was not blind in the usual sense of the word, because he responded normally to small light flashes in various parts of his visual field. Further, when asked, he could track, by pointing with his index finger, a small object that was moved in front of him, but he could never *name* the object that he obviously was seeing and tracking. Now, was this inability to name objects due to a disturbance of linguistic functions? Was he simply aphasic? Although he had an obvious aphasia as well as a number of other cognitive and physical disabilities, none of these deficits seemed to be *sufficient* to explain why he could not name any object placed before him, since he *could* name any object placed in his right or left hand, and say how it was used, about as well as any blindfolded normal subject. Thus, his naming problem was restricted to the visual modality. Was his visual acuity so poor that he couldn't see the object clearly enough to name it? This was easily ruled out by tests of visual acuity. At this point some of you will know that his behavioral deficit is characteristic of a syndrome called visual agnosia, a name coined by Sigmund Freud when he was a young neurologist to indicate merely the loss of visual knowledge.

Members of the medical profession, as you are no doubt aware, are trained to use Latin names to hide their ignorance of what is really wrong with their patients. Although this practice may reassure the patient, Freud was not so naive that he confused a name with an explanation, and he came up with the hypothesis that visual agnosia results from a loss of *visual memories*. Note that this reduction of a number of behavioral deficits to a single impaired cognitive function seems quite plausible and, indeed, it is still considered to be a correct interpretation, at least for some cases of visual agnosia. In the present case, however, such an explanation seems unlikely since the patient could describe many objects from memory—a shoebox, a telephone and its usual color (at that time almost always black), a hammer, a basketball, a hockey stick, a key ring, and so on. But immediately after describing such an object from memory he could not name it when it was shown to him. Further, if he was shown a *moving* key ring and asked to describe it, he only could say he saw something "shiny," but could not name it until the keys were jingled. As soon as he heard the sound he instantly shot out the name "keys." He could not recognize any of the ward staff or his physicians until they spoke, and, on hearing them speak, he addressed them by their correct names. He also could not identify his wife, a photograph of himself or even himself in a mirror, a syndrome called prosopagnosia, another non-explanatory Latin term to say that a patient cannot recognize even familiar faces.

Despite the extensive brain damage he suffered, the patient was aware that something was wrong with his vision, and this awareness was reflected not only in his verbal communications, but also in his *dreams*: He had a recurrent nightmare in which he was in a sealed dark barrel from which he couldn't escape: The barrel was tumbling over Niagara Falls and he could hear the noise and people yelling for him to get out. This dream gives some insight into the horrifying emotional impact that cognitive deficits can have on a patient.

Quite determined to discover what was wrong with this patient, I spent many months devising various tests of his visual behavior. It soon became obvious that he could not find or point to any object that was *not* in motion with respect to a complex visual background. Here are two examples: When brought to my office in a wheel chair, he was totally unaware that I was sitting in my chair if I didn't move. If I did move and was wearing a white coat, he'd say, "Hi, doc," but he still did not recognize me until I spoke. The second example involved placing various objects on a colored advertisement torn from a Sears, Roebuck catalogue in such a way that he could not see me doing it. I then would ask him to point to the "thing" on the piece of paper. He *never succeeded*. However, if I jiggled the advertisement so that the object moved with respect to the background he *never failed*: His hand shot out instantly and he touched it accurately. Although I would not maintain that he had a normal level of intelligence, it was clear that he exhibited some ability to make deductions on the basis of visual input: For example, I taught him, one at a time, the names of some 20 common objects (scissors, pencil, paper clip, etc.) each time keeping the object in motion against the advertisement. After several days of practice he could unfailingly apply the correct name to each of these moving objects by making use of one or more distinctive features such as its reflectance, size, or color.

One of these objects was a playing card that had a complex pattern in red and white. He had been taught to call this a playing card, and he had always seen only its back, the red and white pattern, while I kept it in motion on the colored advertisement. One day I substituted a small red and white postage stamp. A wry smile crossed his face, indicating that he recognized the trick, and he said, "Oh, that's a piece of a playing card." Since he clearly could name colors, and had a good sense of the size of an object, his response, a *piece* of a playing card, indicated that he could utilize the information available to him and come up with an intelligent, albeit incorrect, inference.

At this point, one might reasonably conclude that his fundamental cognitive deficit was an inability to distinguish figure from background. Indeed, as long ago as World War I, Poppelreuter (1917) showed soldiers, with gunshot wounds of the occipital cortex, overlapping line drawings of common objects. Figure 3 is one of Poppelreuter's drawings. These patients had great difficulty in finding a named object in such a jumble and for many years neurologists carried one or more such figures in their medical bags since they were reasonably reliable in diagnosing occipital lesions in the

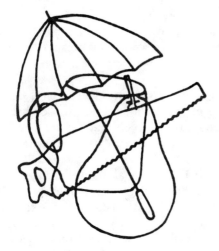

FIGURE 3. Overlapping line drawing by Poppelreuter (1917). From Walsh, K.W. (1978), *Neuropsychology: A Clinical Approach.* Reproduced by permission of Churchill Livingstone, Edinburgh.

days before CAT and MRI scans. Although my patient undoubtedly had a problem with figure- ground discrimination, would it have been correct to say that *all* his visual disturbances could be explained by (i.e., reduced to) this deficit of figure- ground discrimination? I think this would have been an error. Even when the figure-ground problem was *overcome* by moving the object against the background, so that he could see and point to it, he still did not know what it was — except for the 20 objects he had been taught to name by virtue of the distinctive features of color, size, or reflectance.

In thinking more about this issue, it seemed possible to me that the patient could not name the object even when he saw it moving because he could not determine one other key attribute of an object, its *shape*. This hypothesis was tested in a number of ways. The patient was shown the series of Pseudoisochromatic test plates that are widely used to evaluate color vision. Each of these plates contains a large number of circles of varying sizes, and shades of gray. In addition, each card contains two simple geometrical shapes (crosses, circles, triangles), created by replacing some of these circular gray patches with colored ones, also of varying saturation. The subject is usually required to name the two shapes on each plate, shapes which perceptually pop out of the background by virtue of their color, if the the subject has normal color vision. When my patient was asked what he saw on each plate, he invariably named the color correctly (indicating that his color vision was normal), but he was never able to name or even trace the outlines of the two shapes. Furthermore, when very simple geometrical shapes, such as squares, circles, or triangles were slowly drawn in front of him so that he could see the *movement* of the tip of the pen, he frequently named the shape, but when he was shown the same drawing a few moments later, he could no longer identify it. In another test, the patient was asked to report whether two objects of identical area on a blank background, as seen in Fig. 4, were the same or different. Only when presented with a square and a very long, thin, rectangle was he able to report reliably that they were different.

These, as well as other studies, showed that he had virtually no capacity to discriminate objects on the basis of their *shape* in the visual modality. A good argument can be made, I think, for the hypothesis that a single deficit in visual shape perception accounted for *all* his other visual behavioral deficits: Without the ability to perceive shape, you cannot distinguish figure from background without relative motion, and when it can be distinguished from the background by introducing relative motion you still do not know what it is, and therefore cannot name it. This hypothesis of a single disorder of shape perception might account for the prosopagnosia too, since faces, perhaps more so than any other objects, are recognized by virtue of subtle differences in shape. However, because there are *other* patients with prosopagnosia who do not have a deficit in shape perception, it is not possible at the present time to reject the alternate hypothesis that my patient had *two* independent and unrelated cognitive deficits — one for shape perception and the other for face recognition. One could even argue that he had *three* simultaneously occurring but independent cognitive deficits: shape perception, face recognition, and figure-ground discrimination.

It is obvious that I raise these alternatives to make a point: Here we have a demonstrable visual *perceptual* problem, and even at this low cognitive level it is extremely difficult to apply Occam's Razor, that is, to account for the patient's problem with the *fewest* possible number of hypothesized cognitive functions.

Now why does the clinical neuropsychologist have to use Occam's Razor at all? The answer is obvious: If we don't we are left only with a very large

TEST OF SHAPE PERCEPTION

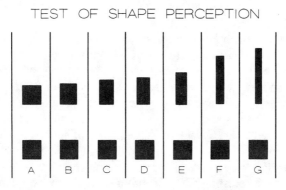

FIGURE 4. Panels A through G each contain two shapes of equal area. The shapes were identical only in Panel A. The subject was required to report if the two shapes presented on a trial were the same or different. The performance of the patient with visual agnosia was above chance levels only for the shapes in Panels F and G.

list of different *tasks* that the patient fails to perform or performs poorly, and we can never conceptually isolate an impaired *cognitive function*. Although it is extremely difficult and risky to identify an impaired cognitive function, the alternative—listing all the behavioral deficits on different tasks—is obviously heuristically sterile.

TIME AND LANGUAGE

I have just indicated how difficult it is to reduce the *perceptual* deficits of visual agnosia and prosopagnosia to a single disturbed function. I now want to illustrate the nature of the problems one faces when the deficits are not perceptual but involve still "higher" levels of cognitive function. In the late 1950s I was studying the inhibitory neurophysiological mechanisms that bring epileptic seizures to an end. In the course of taking many careful neurological histories on patients with epilepsy, I was struck by the frequency with which seizures beginning in the left temporal lobe, that is, in the area of the language centers, gave rise to various subjective disturbances of *time sense* during the aura preceding the epileptic seizure. Time seems to be passing either in slow motion or exceedingly rapidly, events seem to be out of order, or the patient may have particularly intense experiences of *déjà vu* or clairvoyance. In addition, seizures originating in the same anatomical region often are accompanied by a transient aphasia.

These observations led me to speculate on the possible reasons why functional disorders of the time sense and language might be associated. It seemed to me that language is inherently a *temporal* activity: Words in every language are composed of a small sub-set of sounds (the entire set is usually less than 40 in any language) uttered in a particular temporal order; sentences convey meaning because of the particular temporal order of the words which they contain; and a set of sentences also conveys the intended meaning only by virtue of temporal order. This is true, of course, for both written and spoken language. Wielding Occam's Razor deftly, I asked, why should there be *two* independent sets of neural circuits, one used to make judgments about the sequence of a series of events in the environment, and another just used to keep track of the sequence of sounds in a word and the sequence of words in a sentence? Wouldn't it be more parsimonious to assume that the *same* neural circuits supported both functions? And wouldn't it be interesting if these timing circuits were *anatomically co-extensive*? If the left-hemisphere circuits that support language function were the *same* ones as those that keep track of the temporal order of events and the sequence of muscular contractions needed to enunciate words, then damage to these circuits or an epileptic seizure involving them would be expected to result in some significant disturbance of *both* cognitive activities.

Obviously the first step in testing this hypothesis was to devise a way to discover the location of the circuits supporting the capacity to tell the temporal order of two events (Efron, 1963a). The simple principle underlying this method is illustrated in Fig. 5, using an example from astronomy, where two supernovae have exploded simultaneously. Since light waves travel with the same velocity in all directions, an observer located to the left of the plane half-way between the two explosions will see the light from supernova #1 before that of supernova #2 and will report that supernova #1 exploded first. Obviously, an observer located on the other side of the plane will report the reverse sequence of events. Only observers located on the plane will report that the two explosions were simultaneous. However, since *we* know that the explosions were simultaneous, the observer's location in space can be deduced from his report of the temporal sequence of events. I thought that this principle could be used to determine the location of the "observer" in the brain.

I was aware of an experiment by Klemm (1925), illustrated in Fig. 6, that

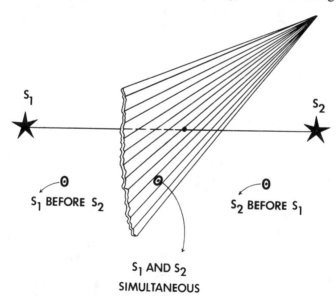

S_1 AND S_2
SIMULTANEOUS

FIGURE 5. Inferring the location of an observer from his report of the temporal sequence of two events. S1 and S2 represent supernovae that have exploded simultaneously. An observer located to the left of the plane equidistant from the two explosions will report that S1 exploded before S2. An observer located to the right of the plane will give the opposite report. From the report given, one can locate the position of the observer.

could be adapted for my purpose. Klemm gave weak electrical shocks to the forehead and toe of subjects and found that when the two shocks were simultaneous, the subjects reported that the forehead shock preceded the toe shock. It was only when the toe shock, which set up impulses that had further to travel to the brain, was given *before* the forehead shock that his subjects reported the two shocks to be simultaneous. Although Klemm's experiment only tells us that the "observer" is located closer to the forehead than to the toe, hardly a surprise, his method of using judgments of simultaneity was just what I needed.

The two experiments I performed are illustrated in Fig. 7. In the first, equally intense shocks were given to the right and left index finger tips of neurologically normal subjects. In the second, equally bright lights were flashed in the right and left half-fields. Thus the shocks and light flashes were presented in such a way that one was projected to the right hemisphere and the other to the left. In each experiment I varied the order and interval between the two stimuli and merely required the subjects to report if they were simultaneous or not. Assuming that I was very careful to use equally intense stimuli and positioned them carefully, so that the conduction time to the brain would be the same (the biological equivalent of the constant speed of light), I should be able to tell from the subjects' reports whether the "observer" in their brain was closer (in terms of neural conduction time) to the right- or left-sided stimuli, or was equidistant from the right- and left-sided events, as implied by Descartes' theory in which the Soul was located in a midline structure—the pineal gland.

FIGURE 6. An experimental paradigm used by Klemm (1925). With simultaneous shocks delivered to toe and forehead the latter is perceived as occurring first. Subjective simultaneity is achieved only when the toe shock precedes the forehead shock.

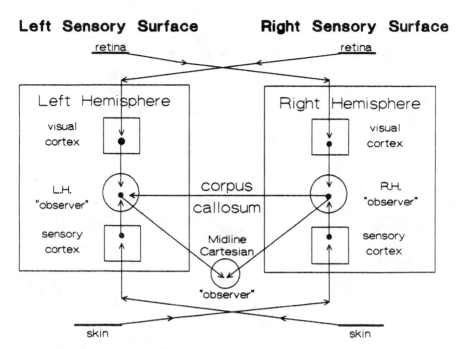

FIGURE 7.   Schematic diagram of neural connections from retina (top) and from skin surface (bottom) to the hypothetical observer located somewhere in the brain. The observer might be located in a midline structure, *equidistant* in terms of transmission time from the right and left sensory surfaces, e.g., in the pineal gland — referred to as a Cartesian observer in his honor because he located the Soul there. The diagram also illustrates an observer located in the right or left hemisphere in which case the transmission time to it from the right- and left-sided stimuli would not be equal. The experiment described in text was aimed at localizing the observer.

The results for both sensory modalities showed that Descartes was wrong! In right-handed subjects the stimuli were reported as being simultaneous when the one projected to the right hemisphere *preceded* the one projected to the left hemisphere by about 4-6 milliseconds. This finding suggested that the observer is located somewhere to the *left* of the midline, because it took the neural message delivered to the right hemisphere 4-6 milliseconds longer to reach it. Electrophysiological evidence available at the time these experiments were performed indicated that a weak electrical shock delivered to the cerebral cortex in one hemisphere produces an electrical response in the mirror image region of the other hemisphere in about 5-6 milliseconds. Putting two and two together, and desperately hoping that I would not get five, I concluded that the observer was located *somewhere* in the left hemisphere and that the information received by the *right* hemisphere was *delayed* by just about the right amount of time necessary for it to be relayed via the corpus callosum to "the observer" in the left hemisphere.

Obviously, this experiment in right-handed subjects provided no information concerning the location of the observer *within* the left hemisphere. Was it anywhere near the left hemisphere language centers? In this respect, the data from the left-handed subjects were interestingly ambiguous: In brief, some of them seemed to have an observer located in the left hemisphere whereas others seemed to have one in the right hemisphere. Since neurological studies of left-sided temporal lobe strokes in left-handed subjects have shown that only about half of them exhibit any signs of aphasia, the results on the left-handed subjects were at least *consistent* with the possibility that the observer might be located right smack in the middle of a subject's speech centers — whether these centers were in the right or left hemisphere. A more direct test of this hypothesis was required.

If the observer and the speech centers are anatomically co-extensive, then an individual with damage to his speech centers should also have a damaged observer, and this in turn might be reflected as a disturbance in the ability to report the correct temporal order of two stimuli, even non-linguistic ones. To test this I performed the following experiments in patients with cerebral lesions (Efron, 1963b): In the first, they were presented with brief red and green light flashes located at the fovea; in the second they were presented with brief high and low pitch sounds from a loud- speaker directly in front of them. For each modality the subjects were required to report the temporal order of the two stimuli. The interval between the two stimuli was varied between 0 and 600 milliseconds. Two groups of subjects were used: patients with left-hemisphere strokes with a relatively moderate aphasia (those with a severe aphasia could not be made to understand the instructions) and patients with strokes but without aphasia, of which only one had had a left-sided stroke. The results were dramatic: The group of patients *with* aphasia had a marked disturbance in performing this task, requiring much longer intervals between the two stimuli to reliably report the correct temporal order than the patients without aphasia. However, the patients with lesions in the roughly comparable region of the right hemisphere were also impaired on this task, as compared to normal subjects, although appreciably less so than the aphasic subjects. It seemed that my initial suspicion might be correct: The neural circuits in the left fronto-temporal area that support language functions appeared to be anatomically co-extensive with those that support temporal order judgments.

The feeling of elation that I experienced, particularly when a number of investigators confirmed and extended my findings of a deficit in temporal order judgments in aphasic subjects, is most accurately conveyed in Fig. 8.

Figure 8 also communicates another feeling, that of despair, which followed when I realized that I had not established any *causal relationship* between the deficit in temporal order judgments and the language deficit but merely an *association* between them. But, while *I* was frustrated by my failure to explain the aphasic language disturbance as damage to the physiological mechanisms that support the ability to keep track of the sequence of events, neuropsychologists were enthusiastic because another task had been discovered that was more impaired following a left- than a right-hemisphere lesion. Ignoring the fact that right-hemisphere damaged patients were also impaired, *they* concluded that my experiments had demonstrated the existence of another cognitive *function*, since referred to as temporal or sequential analysis, for which the left hemisphere is "specialized." And this is how "temporal analysis" ended up on the list of "specialized" left-hemispheric functions with which I began this chapter!

INFERRING HEMISPHERIC "SPECIALIZATIONS" IN NORMAL SUBJECTS

The unseemly haste with which the results of my experiments were added to the rapidly growing list of left-hemispheric specializations alerted me that

"By God, for a minute there it suddenly all made sense!"

FIGURE 8. Drawing by Gahan Wilson; copyright 1986. Reproduced by permission The *New Yorker* Magazine, Inc.

any report of a right/left performance asymmetry would inevitably suffer the same fate. The highly favorable response to my papers was an early warning sign, I thought, that the burden of proof was rapidly shifting to one in which the investigator would have to demonstrate that any right/left performance asymmetry he had found in a cognitive task was *not* a manifestation of a hemispheric "specialization": He would face the impossible task of having to prove the negative. This suspicion proved to be prophetic!

The most dramatic evidence confirming this prophesy can be seen in the huge body of research whose explicitly stated goal is to infer hemispheric specialization for various cognitive functions in *neurologically intact subjects*. Although cognitive psychologists had used normal subjects in their studies for many years, the first *concerted* attempt to infer hemispheric specialization of cognitive functions in normal subjects began with a series of papers by Kimura in the 1960s (1961a; 1961b; 1964; 1967).

Kimura's conclusions had such a major effect on *all* subsequent research on hemispheric specializations that a brief summary of her work is essential. Kimura used a technique, originally invented by Broadbent (1954), now universally known as "dichotic listening," in which two *different* acoustic signals are presented *simultaneously* to the right and left ears using earphones. As can be seen in Fig. 9, one series of spoken digits, for example 1-8-9 is delivered to one ear at the same time that another, say 6-3-4 is presented to the other ear. The subjects' task is to report all the digits heard in any order they wish. When this task was given to patients with lesions in the temporal lobe, before and after unilateral lobectomies that spared the primary auditory cortex, they exhibited a modest post-operative decrease in the number of digits reported from the ear *contralateral* to the lobectomy.

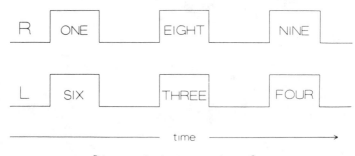

"Name all digits you heard"

FIGURE 9. Diagrammatic representation of the dichotic listening procedure of Kimura. Three spoken digits (one, eight, and nine) presented to the right ear via earphones simultaneously with three digits (six, three, and four) presented to the left ear. The abscissa represents time.

The decreased contralateral performance was more marked, however, in those patients who had a *left* rather than a right temporal lobectomy.

Kimura also made use of another technique, which had just been introduced in Montreal by Wada and Rasmussen (1960), in which a rapid injection of a barbiturate into one or another carotid artery goes initially to one hemisphere and, so to speak, "puts it to sleep" briefly. When injected into the carotid on the side of the individual's so-called "dominant" hemisphere he develops a transient aphasia. Correlating the subject's performance on the dichotic listening task with the side of injection that resulted in transient aphasia, Kimura reported that patients with left-sided speech centers, the usual location in right-handed subjects, tended to have higher recognition scores for the digits presented to the right ear, whereas patients with right-sided speech centers tended to have better performance for the digits played to their left ear. Finally, a group of normal right-handed subjects, whose speech centers would be expected to be located in the left hemisphere, exhibited a superior performance in recognizing the words delivered to the right ear than those to the left ear. In sum, Kimura found that the ear superiority with dichotic presentation of words was *correlated* with the hemisphere which, when anesthetized, produced an aphasia. Clearly, the next step was to explain this correlation.

Unlike the visual system, where information presented to one visual *half-field* is sent to the visual cortex in the opposite hemisphere, in the human auditory system information presented to *one ear* is sent to the auditory cortex in *both* hemispheres. Because each hemisphere receives input from both ears, the destruction of one auditory cortex does not result in deafness of the opposite ear. Why then should there be a right-ear superiority for dichotically presented speech sounds? Kimura (1967) based her explanation on physiological evidence (Rosenzweig, 1951; Tunturi, 1946) in cats and dogs that the electrophysiological response in each auditory cortex is slightly larger for a *click* delivered to the opposite ear than for one delivered to the ear on the same side. She said, "The explanation for the right-ear superiority on the digits test, then, was that the right ear had better connections with the left hemisphere than did the left ear, and since the left hemisphere was the one in which speech sounds were presumably analyzed, the right-ear sounds had the advantage of having better access to these speech centers. In the case where speech is represented in the right hemisphere, however, the opposite pattern of ear-superiority should occur, since here it is the left ear which has the favoured connections" (p. 164). This has come to be known as the direct/indirect access theory.

Kimura was also aware, however, that the difference between the ipsilateral and contralateral physiological response to clicks was small, and she adopted Rosenzweig's suggestion that the stronger response in the primary auditory cortex produced by the contralateral signal might partially "occlude" or "suppress" the information from the weaker ipsilateral stimulus—in effect making it still weaker functionally. Although this occlusion or suppression effect would be present in *both* auditory cortices, the *unsuppressed* information from the right ear would have *direct access* to the centers in the left hemisphere that are specialized for language, whereas the unsuppressed left-ear information in the right hemisphere would have only *indirect access* to the left hemisphere language centers via the corpus callosum. Because the unsuppressed auditory information in the right auditory cortex had a longer path to reach the language center in the left hemisphere, Kimura assumed that it would be somewhat degraded. Thus in the dichotic listening paradigm it was assumed that the language centers in the left hemisphere directly receive non-degraded, unsuppressed information from the *right* ear and indirectly receive degraded, unsuppressed information from the *left* ear.

In 1964 Kimura provided what then appeared to be the clinching piece of evidence that her assumptions were valid: Neurologists previously had noted that impaired performance in some musical tasks was more common with right- than with left-hemisphere damage. By the 1960s this was expressed in the prevailing jargon as a right hemispheric "specialization" for music. If her assumptions were correct, and two different *musical passages* were presented dichotically, a *left*-ear superiority would be expected. Using dichotically presented Baroque melodies, Kimura reported a *left*-ear recognition superiority in normal subjects. This later report appears to have convinced many investigators that by using the dichotic listening technique with the appropriate material, one could infer the hemisphere which was specialized for performing any auditory task. This conviction was reinforced by two reports in 1968 (Milner, Taylor, & Sperry, 1968, and Sparks & Geschwind, 1968) that split-brain subjects reported very few of the spoken digits presented to the left ear, and some of them claimed that they heard *nothing* in the left earphone at all. These experiments seemed to confirm the validity of Kimura's second assumption of a suppression of the weaker ipsilateral auditory signal by the stronger contralateral signal in each hemisphere: The split-brain subjects appeared to be deaf for digits presented to their left ear when other digits were presented simultaneously to their right ear, but heard the digits *normally* in their left ear when there were *no* digits presented in the right ear.

It seemed obvious that Kimura's reasoning should be as applicable to the visual as to the auditory system. Indeed, because of the anatomy of the visual system the suppression assumption was not even required. All one needed was the first assumption—of differential access to the hemisphere that was "specialized" to perform the task. The direct/indirect access assumption appeared to explain the much earlier observations of others that words and letters presented to the right visual half-field, and thus directly projected to the left hemisphere, were recognized with higher accuracy or with a shorter reaction time than those projected to the left visual half-field and then presumably transmitted with degradation to the left-hemisphere language center.

IMPACT OF THE DIRECT/INDIRECT
ACCESS THEORY

Kimura's work had a major impact in four respects. *First*, it convinced many investigators that the simultaneous presentation of different categories of information to the two ears, the two visual half-fields, or the two sides of the skin surface offered a powerful method by which they could identify many different types of hemispheric specializations in a readily available *normal* population whose performance would not be contaminated or obscured by the effects of brain damage.

Second, it created a thriving "low-tech" cottage industry in which all one needed was a cheap two-channel tape recorder and/or slide projector with a shutter and a little bit of electricity. What previously had been a well-guarded academic preserve of a few neurologists and neuropsychologists having access to patients with rare neurological lesions had now opened up, more democratically, to anyone with an interest in the subject of hemispheric specialization.

The *third* major impact of Kimura's work was that she redefined the concept of "specialization." Prior to her work, the cognitive function of a brain region, its specialization, had been defined in terms of the symptoms produced when it was damaged. But even this *flawed* definition of "specialization" is *inapplicable* to the normal subject who has no cerebral damage. Instead of using *symptoms* to define the specialized cognitive function of a damaged cerebral area, Kimura used the *right/left performance asymmetry* to define the specialized cognitive function of an undamaged hemisphere: In essence, *the performance asymmetry now became the symptom*. If a dichotic listening or a tachistoscopic experiment in normal subjects revealed a left-ear or a left visual half-field superiority, then this operationally defined the existence of a right-*hemispheric* specialization for the task. Conversely, a right-ear or a right visual half-field performance superiority constituted *prima facie* evidence for a left-*hemispheric* specialization. The word "hemispheric" has been emphasized in the two preceding sentences to call attention to the fact that with these methods, the localization of the purported cognitive function could be assigned to no anatomical region smaller than an entire hemisphere.

The *last* major reason for the enthusiasm was the guaranteed success of *any* experiment with these methods. This assurance of success is a direct logical consequence of the new way of defining cognitive specializations.

Let me amplify: In such experiments there are only three possible results, *and every one is publishable*! Using some type of visual, tactile, or auditory material, one *must* find a right, left or no performance superiority — there is no other possible outcome. Whatever the result, an important contribution to the field of laterality research had been made, which, of course, necessarily leads to further experiments, each with a similarly guaranteed outcome. And, performing experiments with such a guaranteed outcome also improves one's chances of obtaining academic tenure!

A simple example should suffice: If an experiment demonstrated a *left* visual field performance superiority in recognizing, detecting or reporting some *novel* type of visual shape or pattern, this provided critically important "converging evidence" further defining the precise characteristics of the already-claimed right-hemispheric superiority for visual-spatial functions. However, if the experiment gave rise to the opposite result, this would be particularly worth publishing because it would mean that the *left* hemisphere is specialized for the processing of the *particular* visual-spatial stimuli that were used in that experiment. Finally, if no asymmetry was observed, this too would be important evidence that for the *particular* visual-spatial stimuli used, the two hemispheres are equally "specialized."

This is known on the street as a "win-win-win situation" and had the prophesied result that hundreds of different "hemispheric specializations" were claimed within a relatively short period of time. Thus an investigator might ask, and inevitably one did (Gordon, 1970), whether the left-ear performance superiority in Kimura's experiment that used melodies was truly a reflection of right-hemispheric specialization for all musical tasks or an indication of a right-hemispheric specialization for melodies only. Although he found *no* performance asymmetry when he used dichotically presented melodies and digits, thus *failing to confirm* Kimura's original claims for these two types of stimuli, he did find a weak, but statistically significant, *left*-ear superiority in the recognition of dichotically presented musical chords created with an electric organ. In the field of laterality research even the *failure* to replicate the reports of another investigator has a special status: Unlike other scientific disciplines, where a failure to replicate may be published because it is a possible adverse reflection on the validity of the *initial* claim, in the field of laterality research the failure is usually dismissed by the *later* investigator on the grounds of minor methodological differences! Indeed, since it is almost impossible to duplicate another's experiment exactly, the chronic failure to get the same results in closely similar experiments has been taken as evidence of the exquisite subtlety of hemispheric specializations!

I hate to spoil the party, but it is time to call your attention to the fact that we are dealing with a closed conceptual system resembling the Ptolemaic theory of planetary motions, where any new observation was accounted for by postulating yet another planetary epicycle. In this case, any new experimental observation is accounted for by postulating another, heretofore unrecognized, "hemispheric specialization." In common with other closed conceptual systems, this new way of defining hemispheric specializations *cannot be falsified* by any new right/left performance asymmetry that is discovered. But the most devastating characteristic of such closed theoretical systems is that they inhibit research on alternative explanations of the phenomena or direct tests of the assumptions that are the basis of the system, at least among the "true believers."

The views I expressed in this chapter are not likely to be received enthusiastically by these true believers. Since the *facts* I have presented are indisputable, the only charge that could be leveled against me is that I have made too much of the way words are used in the field of laterality research, and that the arguments I have advanced represent nothing more than a semantic dispute. I have already dealt with the claim that the concept of "specialization" is used merely as a short-hand way of restating the existence of a correlation between the site of a brain lesion and some type of cognitive deficit. Even a cursory reading of the literature reveals that the true believers actually mean that the purported cognitive function had been *performed by* and *in* the piece of brain tissue prior to its damage. When they refer to studies of normal subjects, they actually mean that the purported cognitive function is *performed by* and *in* the hemisphere presumed to be responsible for the superior performance. This is *not* a matter of semantic dispute: Kimura's direct/indirect access theory is *explicitly* and *unambiguously* based on the idea that the purported cognitive function is performed within the hemisphere that has direct access to the relevant information.

The real problem, however, is that we do not at present understand the cognitive function of *any* brain area, let alone an entire hemisphere! For example, what is the cognitive function of the left fronto-temporal cortex, which, when damaged, results in aphasia? And what is the cognitive function of the striate cortex, which, when damaged bilaterally, results in blindness? To declare that these areas are specialized for language and vision respectively is logically equivalent to, *and no less banal* than, the declaration that the legs are specialized for walking since walking is seriously impaired without legs! Unfortunately, when the speaker is referring to that most fascinating of all organs, the brain, the unsophisticated listener, and many neuropsychologists as well, are led to believe that the field of cognitive neuroscience has achieved, to use Chairman Mao's phrase, "A great leap forward."

In the following chapter I will show how this logical error is actually a great lurch *sideways* into a scientific dead end.

2

The Fall of Hemispheric Specialization

INTRODUCTION

In the previous chapter I identified several epistemological problems that have plagued the field of neuropsychology and some of the consequences of the failure to address these adequately. In this chapter I narrow my focus to the problems entailed in inferring hemispheric specialization of cognitive function from the right/left performance asymmetries observed in neurologically normal individuals using the techniques of dichotic listening and tachistoscopic visual presentation. Following Kimura's work in the early 1960s, described at the end of the previous chapter, these asymmetries were considered to be *prima facie* evidence of hemispheric specialization for the particular category of stimuli that had been used in the experiment: words, letters, shapes, melodies, and so forth. In this chapter I will discuss the reasons why this view had to be abandoned, and why the more cautious view that has replaced it also will have to be abandoned.

I maintain that neither of these experimental techniques has so far provided any *independent* evidence that the two hemispheres are differentially specialized for cognitive functions, and that they are most unlikely to do so in the foreseeable future. The most that could possibly be claimed is that a few—a very few—of the findings are consistent with known correlations between brain-lesion site and specific cognitive disturbances, the so-called "converging evidence." When you consider some of the "diverging evidence" that I will describe in this chapter, however, I believe that you will come to share my view that these studies on neurologically normal subjects have not made, and will not in the foreseeable future make, any material contribution to a deeper understanding of hemispheric differences in cognitive function.

DICHOTIC LISTENING EXPERIMENTS

Speech Signals

I will begin with the right-ear superiority for the recognition of dichotically presented speech signals, first reported by Kimura (1961a, 1961b), that has been attributed almost universally to a left-hemispheric specialization for *linguistic* processing. In these experiments various types of natural or synthetic speech sounds have been used: spoken digits, meaningful words, or computer synthesized speech such as consonant-vowel or consonant-vowel-consonant sounds. Regardless of the type of speech stimulus used, it is a fact that marked individual differences in performance are observed: A *left*-ear superiority is not as exceptional as you might think. In various experiments 20% to 45% of right-handed subjects exhibit some degree of *left*-ear superiority; in some of these individuals the left-ear superiority is statistically significant, in others it is not (Blumstein, Goodglass, & Tartter, 1975; Lauter, 1982; Wexler, Halwes, & Heninger, 1981). Although Blumstein et al. obtained a test-retest reliability coefficient of 0.74, 36% of their right-handed subjects exhibited a *left*-ear superiority in at least one of the two sessions and 29% of them switched ear superiority on retesting. In another study (Speaks, Niccum, & Carney, 1982), which used more trials than any other in the literature, only 62.5% of the subjects exhibited a *statistically* significant right- or left-ear superiority, and of those who did, fewer than 80% had a right-ear superiority. Thus, less than 50% of the *entire* population showed a statistically significant performance superiority in the right ear.

Based on the incidence of aphasia in right-handed individuals with right-hemisphere strokes, not more than 1%-3% of right-handed subjects would be expected to have a *right*-hemispheric "specialization" for language. How, then, is this extraordinarily high incidence of aberrant results to be explained? There are only two possibilities: Either the *right* hemisphere in only 50% of right-handed subjects is "specialized for language" to a statistically significant degree, or the dichotic listening technique is at best a very poor *measure* of the hemispheric specialization for language. The first alternative is nothing short of blasphemy: It conflicts with the most sacred tenet of laterality research, left hemispheric "specialization" for language. The second alternative, of course, conflicts directly with the assumption that the right-ear performance superiority provides *prima facie* evidence of hemispheric specialization for language. Given this uncomfortable choice, the field of laterality research has belatedly accepted the second alternative—that there must be some factor or set of factors operating in these aberrant subjects, but not in the majority, that is so powerful that it can counterbalance or even *reverse* the right-ear superiority with dichotically presented speech sounds. Later in this chapter I will discuss the dismaying implications for the field of laterality research that arise once the idea is abandoned that the performance asymmetry provides *prima facie* evidence of hemispheric specialization.

The problem, however, extends well beyond the issue of individual variation, as is evident when I describe the results of a most interesting experiment by Kimura and Folb (1968). They used trisyllabic nonsense speech played forward or backward in a dichotic listening paradigm. They found a comparable right-ear superiority in *both* conditions, with the usual 25% of aberrant subjects, and concluded that "the critical distinguishing characteristics of speech sounds are not related to meaningfulness, familiarity, or conceptual content" (p. 396). Since both meaningful as well as meaningless speech-like sounds give rise to a right-ear performance superiority of the same magnitude, however, a more plausible conclusion might be that a right-ear performance superiority arises when the acoustical signals used have a complex temporal and/or spectral structure.

The same conclusion, based on dichotically presented Morse code—a set of sounds distinguished *only* by their temporal structure—was reached by Papçun, Krashen, Terbeek, Remington and Harshman (1974) in a paper entitled "Is the left hemisphere specialized for speech, language and/or something else?" They found that Morse code operators had a right-ear superiority in the perception of the code. They also found that subjects who did not know Morse code had a right-ear superiority, but only with dot-dash patterns containing seven or less elements. With more than seven elements the naive subjects exhibited a *left*-ear superiority, and the authors speculated that in this more difficult task the naive subjects were forced to "adopt strategies involving the holistic qualities of the stimuli." Their overall conclusion, the "something else" in their clever title, was that the left *hemisphere* is "specialized for processing the sequential parts of which a stimulus is composed." Thus, the right-ear superiority observed with dichotic presentation of *meaningless* speech-like sounds and with Morse Code (a meaningless temporal pattern for the uninitiated) indicates that the right-ear superiority for *meaningful* speech sounds is not necessarily a reflection of a left-hemispheric "specialization" for *language*.

Indeed, there is a considerable body of evidence that the underlying cause of the right-*ear* superiority for "linguistic stimuli" in dichotic listening experiments is the right-*ear* superiority in the processing of acoustic signals having a complex temporal microstructure (Blumstein, Baker, & Goodglass, 1977; Blumstein, Cooper, Zurif, & Caramazza, 1977; Chedru, Bastard, & Efron, 1978; Divenyi & Efron, 1979; Efron 1963a, 1963b; Halperin, Nachshon, & Carmon, 1973; Kimura & Folb, 1968; Lackner & Teuber, 1973; Papçun et al., 1974; Sasanuma, Tatsumi, Kiritani, & Fujisaki, 1973; Swisher & Hirsh, 1972; Tallal & Newcombe, 1978). I cannot emphasize too strongly, however, that it is only if one accepts the key assumption that a performance asymmetry provides *prima facie* evidence for a hemispheric "specialization" that one can conclude that the left *hemisphere* is specialized for temporal analysis. I have already indicated *one* of the reasons why this critical assumption has had to be abandoned: the fact that only 50% of the population exhibits a statistically significant right-ear superiority for dichotically presented speech sounds. The other reasons will emerge shortly.

Pure Tone Signals

My next example does not derive from any study of hemispheric differences in processing capacity, but from a series of experiments performed to find out how the central nervous system processes temporal information when two different stimuli are delivered to a sensory system within such a short time interval that the human observer is not aware of the temporal order of the two events. An example with which you are all personally familiar is the illusion of movement that occurs with the very rapid succession of images flashed on the screen at the cinema. It was in the course of these temporal-order experiments (Efron, 1973; Yund & Efron, 1974) that my colleague Bill Yund and I accidentally discovered a perceptual phenomenon that is of particular relevance to this chapter.

Figure 10 illustrates the experimental paradigm we used. Two brief stimuli, A and B, each only 10 milliseconds in duration, were presented in rapid succession. In the visual experiment stimulus A was a red flash and B was a green one, and they were projected on the fovea of one eye. In the auditory experiment stimulus A was a pure tone of 1500 Hz and B had a frequency of 1900 Hz, and they were presented to one ear. Less than a second later, A and B were presented again, but in a reversed temporal order. Knowing of Isaac Newton's discoveries, you will predict that in the visual experiment the subject will see two yellow flashes, and, in fact, he does. However, the two yellow colors are *not* identical: The yellow produced by a rapid sequence of red-green is a slightly green-yellow, whereas the green-red sequence is perceived as a slightly orange-yellow, the color component that comes second has more of an effect on the perceived color mixture than the first. The identical phenomenon also occurs in the auditory modality, except of course that it is the *frequency* of the temporally trailing sound that has more of an effect on the perceived pitch.

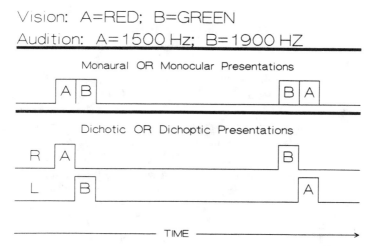

FIGURE 10. Diagrammatic representation of the stimulus presentation. The stimulus parameters for visual and auditory experiments described in text are at the top of figure. The monaural and monocular experiments are illustrated in the middle section; the dichotic and dichoptic experiments are in the lowest section of the figure. The abscissa represents time.

It was evident that we were dealing with a fundamental mechanism involved in the neural integration of rapidly successive stimuli. It was not evident, however, whether this mechanism was in the receptor organ (retina or cochlea) or in the central nervous system. The simplest way to answer this question was to present the stimuli dichoptically and dichotically to see if the perceptual weighting of the trailing stimulus element was present under conditions when the integration could not possibly be at the receptor level. This is illustrated in the lower half of Fig. 10. For both modalities the result was unequivocal. The weighting of the trailing stimulus was the same, proving that the mechanism giving rise to this effect was in the central nervous system.

In these experiments, which were not directed to any issue pertaining to hemispheric differences, one of the conditions involved simultaneous presentations of the two stimulus elements. The visual experiment gave rise to no unexpected results: It made absolutely no difference whether the red flash was projected to the nasal retina of the right eye and the green to the temporal retina of the left eye or the reverse. The yellow colors perceived under these two conditions were indistinguishable. The first trial of the auditory experiment, however, precipitated a laboratory dispute. I happened to be the first subject. Figure 11 illustrates the conditions of that trial. What I heard was a low-pitched sound followed by a high-pitched sound about a second later. My colleague, Bill Yund, obviously had made a mistake and failed to deliver the stimuli to my left ear, and I told him so in no uncertain terms. He was equally vociferous in his denial and quite reasonably suggested that I listen to the signal in each earphone separately. Much to my amazement, and to his as well, there was no instrument problem: It appeared that I was deaf in my left ear and somehow had not noticed it in the 5 previous years during which I was conducting auditory experiments!

Within a few minutes, however, I had my ears tested and much to my relief, my hearing was normal in both ears. I went back to the laboratory and listened again with the same result: I heard only the pitch of the two tones presented to my right ear, but I now noticed something else. The sound images of each dichotic pair of stimuli were not localized in my right *ear* but in the *middle of my head*, a result that could only occur if my brain was receiving equal energy from the two ears. Somehow, my brain was processing the *energy* of the left-ear signals but, apparently, not the *frequency* of those signals.

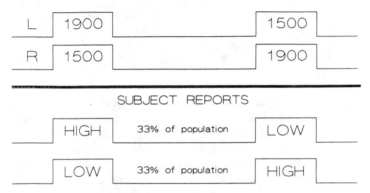

FIGURE 11. Diagrammatic representation of the dichotic lis-tening paradigm with pure tones. On each trial the two ears receive "competing" frequency sequences. The abscissa repre-sents time. In the example illustrated, the left ear receives a high-low frequency sequence simultaneously with a low-high frequency sequence in the right ear. Other trials, at random, contained the reverse frequency sequences in the two ears. In a forced-choice procedure, the subject was required to report which sequence was heard, a high-low or a low-high. With the parameters illustrated in the upper panel, one-third of the population reports the frequency sequence presented to the right ear (a right-ear dominance for pitch), one-third reports the left-ear sequence (a left-ear dominance for pitch), and one-third are equally likely to report the sequence presented to the right or left ear (no significant ear dominance). See text for discussion of the effects of stimulus parameters.

The next step was to reduce the energy progressively in my right ear until I could hear the left-ear pitch information. We then made our second startling discovery: As the energy of the right-ear tones was progressively reduced, the sound image, as expected, shifted to the left earphone. But I still heard only the pitch sequence presented to my *right* ear. And I was hearing it in my *left* ear! Equally startling was the fact that I was hearing the *right*-ear tones not at the *low* intensity level at which they were delivered, but at the *high* intensity level of the left-ear signals — whose pitch I was *not* hearing. This phenomenon could only come about if the frequency and intensity of a signal delivered to each ear were dealt with by two separate neural mechanisms and subsequently recombined. It was not until the right-ear signal was about 40 decibels less intense than the one in my left ear that the two sounds in a trial began to sound similar, and it required about a *45* decibel difference before the two sounds were subjectively indistinguishable — nearly a 200-fold difference in energy.

Thus we accidentally discovered three phenomena within an hour: (1) The frequency and intensity information carried by a sinusoidal stimulus are processed separately and then recombined; (2) I have a right ear "dominance" for processing *frequency* information that requires a massive difference of energy to counterbalance; and (3) My processing of the *energy* of the stimuli is nevertheless right/left symmetrical as reflected by my capacity to localize sounds accurately on the basis of the energy difference between the two ears. We thought it prudent to study some more subjects and to perform a number of other experiments before rushing into print with these astounding claims.

It required many additional experiments by the two of us, and a number of collaborators, over a 9-year period to unravel the implications of the discoveries made in that first hour. I will summarize only those that are most pertinent to the themes of this chapter. The first is the effect of the *frequency difference* between the two dichotically presented pure tones. When the frequency difference is small, all subjects hear a single, compact sound-image whose location is determined by the inter-aural intensity differences. As the frequency difference increases, the sound image becomes less compact, and ultimately, when the frequency difference is large, *two* sound images are perceived, one at each earphone. There is considerable individual variation in frequency difference required to produce two spatially separated sound images. In parallel with these changes in the sound image, increasing the frequency difference also tends to increase the proportion of subjects who exhibit a *right*-ear dominance for pitch. Again, marked individual differences exist: 43% of the population exhibited a significant shift of ear dominance toward the *right* ear as the frequency difference was increased from 100 to 400 Hz; 24% of the population exhibited a significant shift of ear dominance toward the *left* ear with this increased frequency difference; and 33% exhibited no significant change of ear dominance (Efron, Koss, & Yund, 1983).

Despite these profound individual differences in the way ear dominance for pitch changes as a function of the frequency difference, the fact was that 80% of normal hearing subjects have a left-ear dominance for pitch processing with dichotic tones of 1650 Hz and 1750 Hz (Efron, Koss, & Yund, 1983; Gregory, 1982). As you might expect, this has been seized on as evidence that the *right* hemisphere is "specialized" for the processing of pure tones. But if that were the case, why does the *left* hemisphere become "specialized" in many subjects when the only stimulus parameter that has changed is the frequency difference between the pure tones? As is all too common in the field of laterality research, this inconvenient evidence against the explanation in terms of hemispheric specializations—the *divergent* evidence—has conveniently been ignored.

The second issue is the effect on the right/left asymmetry of pitch processing of the *center frequency*—the mean frequency of the two different tones—rather than the *frequency difference* of the two tones presented simultaneously. Ear dominance for pitch processing was examined at different center frequencies under conditions in which the ratio of frequency difference to the center frequency was held constant. The results from five subjects who were patient enough (or were paid enough) to complete this protracted and tedious experiment are illustrated in Fig. 12. Subject RE is me, and it is evident that I have a strong right-ear dominance for pitch processing at all center frequencies between 200 and 4800 Hz. Subject PD exhibited a left-ear dominance at all center frequencies. However, subject BY had a *left*-ear dominance between 200 Hz and 2400 Hz but was strongly *right*-ear dominant at 3200 and 4800 Hz. Subjects LE and MB also exhibited major *reversals* of ear dominance for pitch in different regions of the auditory spectrum (Divenyi, Efron, & Yund, 1977).

Only someone who is unusually credulous could believe that such large and reproducible reversals in ear dominance at different frequencies in an individual arise from reversals in hemispheric specialization! Quite clearly, the robust right/left performance asymmetries for dichotically presented pure tones—the phenomenon of ear dominance for pitch—must be explained differently.

The fact that ear dominance in an individual subject could change as a function of the frequency difference between dichotically presented pure tones and the center frequency of such a pair of tones led us to develop a mathematical model of ear dominance for pitch, which included only cochlear and early brain stem pitch processing mechanisms (Yund & Efron, 1977). We then designed a number of experiments to test the assumptions of this model and to see if we could *predict* the changes of ear dominance in

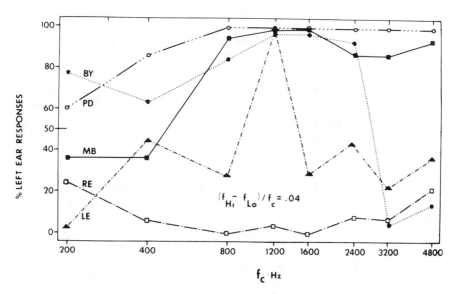

FIGURE 12.   The effect on ear dominance for pitch as a function of the center frequency of the dichotic tone pair. The center frequency is on the abscissa. The ordinate represents the percentage of trials in which the subject reported the frequency sequence delivered to the left ear, with values above 50% reflecting left-ear dominance and values below 50% reflecting right-ear dominance. The ratio of the difference between the high and low frequencies divided by the center frequency was constant (0.04) at all center frequencies. Data of 5 subjects. See text for discussion. Reproduced from Divenyi, Efron, and Yund (1977) by permission of *Journal Acoustical Society of America* and the authors.

individual subjects on the basis of measured parameters of their auditory system.

In brief, we found the following: (1) Monaurally measured frequency discrimination is superior in the ear that is dominant for pitch in the dichotic paradigm: A single psychoacoustic parameter (the relative steepness of the frequency tuning function of the two ears) accounts for the agreement between the monaural frequency discrimination and the dichotic ear dominance for pitch (Divenyi, Efron, & Yund, 1977). (2) For dichotic stimuli having equal intensities in the two ears, ear dominance in an individual subject varies with stimulus intensity. Measurements of the *shape* of the intensity-response transduction function in each ear allowed us to predict these changes in magnitude and direction of ear dominance in individual subjects (Efron, Yund, & Divenyi, 1979). Furthermore, measurements of the shape of the intensity-response transduction function in subjects with cochlear sensory-neural hearing loss are now being used in our laboratory to determine the amplification parameters at each frequency for a multichannel hearing aid. The effectiveness of this hearing aid in the initial studies also supports the validity of the model (Yund, Simon, & Efron, 1987). (3) As mentioned in the earlier description of my own behavior, a very large decrease in the intensity of the right-ear tone is required to overcome my right-ear dominance for pitch. At these interaural intensity differences the model predicts that the bone conducted information from the more intense left-ear signal to my right cochlea should be a critical factor in determining the interaural intensity difference at which my ear dominance is overcome. By using insertion earphones, which reduce the amount of bone conduction from one earphone to the opposite cochlea, an even larger interaural intensity difference was needed to overcome my ear dominance for pitch. We confirmed this result on other subjects with right- and left-ear dominance (Yund, Efron, & Divenyi, 1979).

All these findings indicate that ear dominance for pitch arises from asymmetries in the *peripheral* auditory system. In the context of this discussion I use the term "peripheral" to mean at or below the level of the brain-stem. You should be alerted to the fact that a number of electrophysiological studies of brain-stem evoked potentials have revealed right/left asymmetries (e.g., Berlin, Allen, & Parrish, 1981; Bopanna & Moushegian, 1988; Chiappa, Gladstone, & Young, 1979; Decker & Howe, 1981; Dobie & Berlin, 1979). One of these studies is illustrated in Fig. 13, in which a 500 Hz tone was delivered to the right *or* left ear of subjects with normal hearing and symmetrical right/left auditory thresholds. A right/left asymmetry in the amplitude and latency of the frequency following response (which arises in the brain-stem) was present in all 10 of the subjects tested. Six of them, like the subject shown in Fig. 13, exhibited a more pronounced response for right-ear stimuli, whereas the remaining four had more marked left-ear responses.

The role that these brain-stem evoked potential asymmetries in normal subjects may play in dichotic listening experiments remains to be elucidated. Their existence, however, should serve as a warning that we know too little at the present time to accept the wide-spread assumption that asymmetries in dichotic listening experiments reflect *hemispheric* levels of cognitive activity. A very large part of the auditory system lies below the hemisphere!

Dichotic Experiments on Split-Brain Subjects

If ear dominance for pitch arises from peripheral rather than hemispheric auditory asymmetries, then split-brain subjects should behave just like normal individuals in dichotic pure-tone experiments. This prediction was tested in a collaborative experiment with J.E. Bogen, the neurosurgeon who

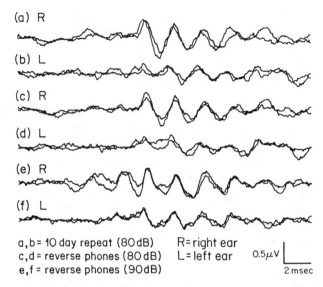

a,b = 10 day repeat (80 dB)   R = right ear
c,d = reverse phones (80 dB)   L = left ear   0.5μV
e,f = reverse phones (90 dB)   2 msec

FIGURE 13. Evoked potentials reflecting the frequency following response (FFR) to a 500 HZ tone presented monaurally. The two superimposed traces reflect data obtained 10 days apart. Note the larger amplitude FFR in this subject for right ear stimulation. See text for discussion. Reproduced by kind permission of B. Bopanna and G. Moushegian.

performed many of the commissurotomies on the patients reported by Sperry and his associates. Since the rationale of our experiment was modeled on that used in split-brain subjects by Milner, Taylor and Sperry (1968), I describe their experiments first.

In their first experiment they used the dichotic listening paradigm developed by Kimura and illustrated in Fig. 9. The split-brain subjects rarely named any of the digits presented to the left ear, and some reported that they heard nothing at all in the left earphone. The authors interpreted these findings as strong evidence supporting Kimura's assumption that, within each hemisphere, the signal from the contralateral ear suppresses the input from the ipsilateral ear (see discussion of Kimura's suppression assumption in the previous chapter). They recognized, of course, that in subjects whose right hemisphere was disconnected from the left, the presumed *un*suppressed signal in the *right* hemisphere could not reach the language centers in the left hemisphere, and this would prevent the subject from naming the digits presented to their left ear; requiring the digits to be *named* assesses only the left hemisphere's behavior. Their second experiment was designed to determine whether the same suppression was present also in the right hemisphere. While the subjects sat before a number of objects that were screened from view, they heard two dichotically presented messages, for example, "Now pick up the paper clip" in one ear at the same time as "Now find us the eraser" in the other ear. To assess the right hemisphere's behavior, the subjects were required to pick up with the *left hand* the object that was named. The authors reported that the "Scores for left-hand retrieval under these conditions showed a strong preference for objects named through the left ear, with a partial to complete neglect of items named through the right ear. When asked to name the left-ear items picked up with the left hand, the subjects commonly misnamed the objects, using the names that were presented simultaneously through the right ear" (p. 185). These findings, with *linguistic* stimuli, were attributed to a nearly complete suppression of the ipsilateral by the contralateral input that occurs in *both* hemispheres.

At this point a parenthetical comment is in order. You may well wonder how a split-brain subject could perform this task at all: To pick up with the *left* hand an object named in the message presented through the left earphone must mean that the neurosurgically isolated *right* hemisphere could understand speech! Furthermore, the right hemisphere must have understood the verbally presented instructions governing the entire experiment. But how is this to be reconciled with the claim that it is the *left* hemisphere that is specialized for linguistic functions? Clearly, the isolated right hemisphere must be sufficiently specialized for linguistic functions to at least understand the instructions for the experiment and to execute the message. I mention this issue only to remind you of my discussion in Chapter 1 that neural circuits supporting linguistic functions do not reside exclusively in the left hemisphere: Although the right hemisphere may be unable to speak, it apparently understands speech sufficiently well to allow the split-brain subject to execute a verbal command presented to the left ear when a different command is simultaneously presented to the right ear. The degree to which studies of split-brain patients have, in fact, confirmed the existence of right-hemisphere speech is a matter of some debate: Gazzaniga (1983) has claimed, "Indeed, it could well be argued that the cognitive skills of a normal disconnected right hemisphere without language are vastly inferior to the cognitive skills of a chimpanzee" (p.536). Myers (1984), in a detailed review of the data on 21 of Gazzaniga's split-brain patients, asserts that Gazzaniga has seriously misinterpreted the facts. As you might expect, in his rebuttal Gazzaniga (1984) defends his own interpretation. I mention this dispute to alert the reader that many of the conclusions drawn from the study of split-brain patients, and not merely those pertaining to right-hemisphere linguistic competence, are not as convincing as you have been led to believe.

The object of our own experiment in split-brain subjects (Efron, Bogen, & Yund, 1977) was to see if the suppression phenomenon was present also for dichotically presented pure tones. One advantage of using dichotically presented pure tones is that it is possible to vary the perceived spatial separation of the sound images by varying the frequency difference between them. This offered the opportunity to deliver competing pitch sequences to the two ears under conditions in which the right- and left-ear signals were perceived at a *single* location rather than lateralized separately to the two ears. We used pure tones of 1500 and 1900 Hz in the paradigm, illustrated in Fig. 11, since this frequency difference produces a single sound image in normal subjects. The specific question was whether each of the disconnected hemispheres of the split-brain subject would report the pitch sequence delivered to the contralateral ear, thus disregarding the competing signal presented to the ipsilateral ear, just as it does with simultaneously presented, spatially separated speech sounds.

To determine how each hemisphere "heard" the stimuli, the split-brain subjects were asked whether they heard a "high-low" or "low-high" pitch sequence on each trial. In the first experiment the subjects' *verbal* report was used to assess the left hemisphere's perception of the stimuli. In the next two experiments the subjects reported by pointing to an upward arrow (to indicate a "high-low" pitch sequence) or to a downward arrow (to indicate a "low-high" pitch sequence). As in the Milner, Taylor, and Sperry experiment, the manual response of the right hand assessed the left hemisphere's perception of the pitch sequence, while the left-hand response assessed the right hemisphere's perception.

To determine how the perception varied as a function of interaural intensity difference, we used 11 different combinations of signal intensity in the right and left ear. The characteristic psychometric functions obtained in normal subjects for those stimulus parameters are illustrated in Fig. 14. This figure contains five psychometric curves. The R2 curve is typical of a subject with a strong right-ear dominance. The R1 curve exemplifies a subject with a moderate right-ear dominance. The curve denoted with a zero exemplifies an individual with no ear dominance and the curves L1 and L2 reflect subjects with moderate and strong left-ear dominance, respectively. Although only five curves are illustrated in Fig. 14, the magnitude and direction of ear dominance for pitch in a large population of subjects falls on a *continuum* from strong right- to strong left-ear dominance.

The first split-brain subject (LB, in Fig. 15) exhibits the characteristic psychometric function of a normal subject with a moderately strong right-ear dominance for pitch. The two curves in this figure assessing the left hemisphere's perception of the stimuli (verbal and right-hand responses) are identical with the right hemisphere's perception of the same stimuli (left-hand response). Subject NG (Fig. 16) is typical of a strongly right-ear dominant subject. Since this subject could not *name* pitch sequences, even monaurally, but could hum what she heard, we had her hum the responses. Whether this humming response assesses the right or left hemisphere's

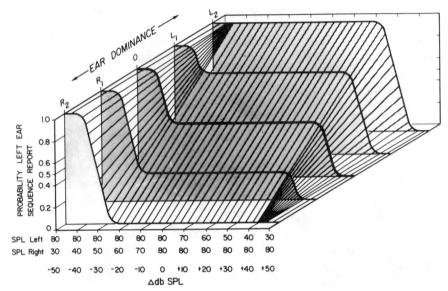

FIGURE 14.   The effect of interaural intensity differences (on the abscissa) in a dichotic pure-tone experiment; the probability of reporting the left-ear frequency sequence on ordinate. Curve R2 is typical of a strongly right-ear-dominant subject; Curve R1 for a moderately right-ear-dominant subject; Curve 0 for a subject without ear dominance; Curve L1 for a moderately left-ear-dominant subject; and Curve L2 for a strongly left-ear-dominant subject. These five curves are part of a continuum (indicated by diagonal lines) of the magnitude and direction of ear dominance in a population. The flat portion of each curve indicates the range of interaural intensity differences over which the the subject's probability of report is unchanged. Reproduced from Efron, Bogen, and Yund (1977) by permission of *Cortex*, Masson Italia Periodici, Milan and the authors.

perception is moot. Nevertheless, as with subject LB, all three psychometric functions are identical. Subject DC (Fig. 17) is typical of a strongly left-ear dominant subject, and again the three psychometric curves are the same.

In sum, the performance of split-brain patients, *regardless of which hemisphere produced the response*, was indistinguishable from that of neurologically normal subjects — indicating that *both* hemispheres perceived the dichotic stimuli identically. In short, there was *no* suppression of the ipsilateral by the contralateral input in either hemisphere. These findings in the split-brain subjects are thus consistent with our previous conclusion that the right/left performance asymmetries observed with pure tone stimuli in normal subjects can be fully accounted for by physiological differences in the *peripheral* auditory system: An ear dominance for pitch can arise from

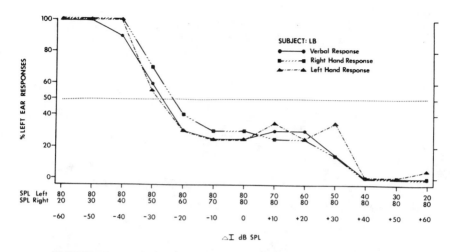

FIGURE 15. Psychometric curves on a split-brain subject with a moderate right-ear dominance for pitch. The curves reflect three different response modes. See text for discussion. Reproduced from Efron, Bogen, and Yund (1977) by permission of *Cortex*, Masson Italia Periodici, Milan and the authors.

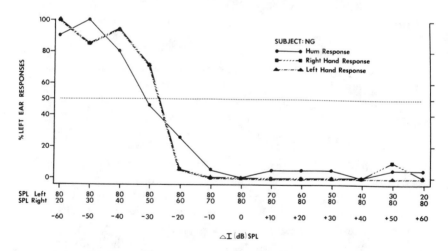

FIGURE 16. Psychometric curves on a split-brain subject with a strong right-ear dominance for pitch. See text for discussion. Reproduced from Efron, Bogen, and Yund (1977) by permission of *Cortex*, Masson Italia Periodici, Milan and the authors.

a right/left difference in the cochlear frequency tuning functions or in the brain-stem where the frequency information from the two ears is combined (Yund & Efron, 1977).

The normal performance of commissurotomized subjects when listening

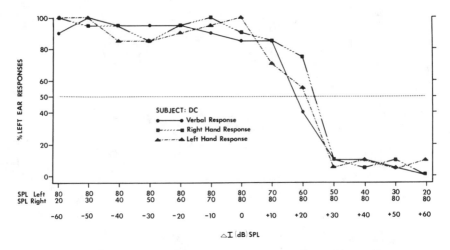

FIGURE 17. Psychometric curves on a split-brain subject with a strong left-ear dominance for pitch. See text for discussion. Reproduced from Efron, Bogen, and Yund (1977) by permission of *Cortex*, Masson Italia Periodici, Milan and the authors.

to dichotic pure tones is markedly different from their behavior when tested with dichotically presented consonant-vowel sounds (/ba/, /da/, /ka/, /pa/, /ta/, /ga/) at equal intensity (Efron, Bogen, & Yund, 1977). LB and NG (who had complete commissurotomies) named the left-ear stimuli at near chance levels, whereas they named all right-ear stimuli correctly. DC (whose splenium was intact) reported somewhat more right- than left-ear stimuli. The results of these experiments thus indicate that a complete commissurotomy has no apparent effect on the perception of dichotically presented pure tones, but has a dramatic one for speech sounds. Why is this the case?

Two possibilities must be considered: The first is that the central auditory system deals with the complex temporal and spectral structure of speech sounds in an entirely different way than with the simple structure of pure tones—the two types of stimuli may be *categorically* different. The second is that the difference arises because the parameters of the pure tone stimuli we used give rise to a *single* sound image, whereas dichotically presented speech sounds produce two spatially separated sound images (one at each earphone) that can be selectively attended. Although this question cannot be answered definitively by the experiments I have just described, a number of experiments by Sparks and Geschwind (1968) on one of the split-brain subjects studied by Sperry and his associates suggest that the second possibility is more likely.

Sparks and Geschwind used the dichotic listening paradigm with spoken digits. As was the case for some of the split-brain subjects studied by Milner et al. (1968), this subject exhibited a failure to name *any* of the digits presented to his left ear. When the identical experiment was repeated, but with instructions to *attend* to the left sound image, left-ear performance improved appreciably, from 0% to 35% correct responses. Clearly, then, the left ear signal was *not* suppressed entirely by physiological processes: Without specific instructions to attend to the digits presented to the left ear this split-brain subject apparently never attended to them.

Their next experiment of interest was to present the digits to the left ear simultaneously with continuous white noise or cocktail party babble in the right ear. The patient now reported, respectively, 100% and 95% of the digits in the left ear under these two conditions: There was no suppression at all, even with *simultaneous* and *physically different* signals in the two ears. Sparks and Geschwind made a point of saying, "The patient recognized the presence of noise on the first test and of confused speech on the second *in the right ear* [my emphasis]" (p. 9). This suggests strongly that, in the presence of a *continuous* acoustic signal located in the right auditory half-field, another (spatially separated) sound image in the left auditory half-field can be attended to perfectly well.

Finally, Sparks and Geschwind presented words dichotically, but with those sent to the *right* ear progressively distorted by filtering out the higher frequency components. The results are illustrated in Table 1. The less the right-ear signal resembles a normal speech sound, the more likely that the left-ear digits are reported. If their data are examined more closely, moreover, a reciprocity relationship is evident: The total number of digits named (right plus left) is nearly constant. This reciprocity relationship has also been described in normal subjects for a dichotic listening experiment using consonant-vowel sounds in which the intensity levels of the right- and left-ear sounds were systematically varied (Berlin et al., 1972). In a subsequent paper one of the authors of that report said, "It must be emphasized again that as one channel was degraded, the performance to the other channel increased. One can add the total information out of both channels and find an almost straight-line 'constant sum'" (Berlin, 1977, p. 307).

The reciprocity relationship seen in the split-brain subject (Sparks &

TABLE 1
Dichotic Digits in Split-Brain Subject Right Ear Frequences Filtered
[Data of Sparks & Geschwind, 1968]

FREQUENCES REMOVED ABOVE:	*PERCENTAGE CORRECT VERBAL REPORTS*		
	LEFT EAR	*RIGHT EAR*	*BOTH EARS*
540HZ	90	15	52.5
780HZ	90	10	50.0
900 HZ	50	70	60.0
1020 HZ	20	100	60.0

Geschwind, 1968) as well as in normal subjects (Berlin et al., 1972) is not easily reconciled with Kimura's assumption of a *physiological* suppression, but is readily accounted for by a tendency to attend more to the right- than the left-sided auditory image, a tendency that is markedly exaggerated following commissurotomy. In our experiments with dichotic pure tones, it will be recalled, there was only a *single* sound image that was randomly located in auditory space by the interaural intensity differences. That sound, wherever located, called attention to itself, what is currently referred to as "exogenous" control of attention. We conclude from these results that in neither hemisphere is there is a *physiological* suppression of the weaker ipsilateral stimulus by the stronger contralateral one, as Kimura, Milner, and others have assumed. Neither hemisphere in the split-brain subject spontaneously attends to the ipsilateral sound image when there are *two* images, one in each auditory half-field. In this respect the split-brain subject is merely exhibiting an exaggeration of the behavior of a normal subject. If this is to be called "suppression," then it is *very* different from the concept of physiological suppression advanced by Kimura (1961a, 1961b).

In this connection, the results of an experiment by Springer, Sidtis, Wilson, and Gazzaniga (1978) is of particular importance. They tested 5 split- brain patients with dichotically presented digits as well as consonant-vowel (CV) sounds. Unlike the split-brain patients reported by Milner et al. (1968) and Sparks and Geschwind (1968), there was only a modest right-ear superiority for the digits — in four of the five patients more than 80% of the left-ear digits were correctly reported. With CV stimuli, on the other hand, the left-ear performance was markedly worse: No subject reported more than 37% of the left ear stimuli, and the mean left-ear performance of the 5 subjects was only 20% (where chance performance would be 16.67%). The authors concluded that the extent of the ipsilateral suppression of the left-ear signal varies as a function of the type of stimulus used and cautioned their readers that, "...it is unwise to assume a comparable degree of ipsilateral suppression of information for all classes of dichotically competing speech stimuli. The results suggest that an important variable may be the degree to which inputs are similar in spectral-temporal micro-structure" (p. 311).

It should be emphasized that CVs became the stimuli of choice for dichotic listening experiments because the critical information in spoken digits is highly redundant. The key phonetic elements of digits therefore cannot, in principle, be perfectly synchronized in the two ears, unlike the consonant elements of the CVs. It is perhaps the *simultaneity* of the consonants in the CV stimuli that is more relevant to an explanation of the Springer et al. results than the similarity of the "spectral-temporal micro-structure." With CV stimuli, the critical information required to identify both stimuli is simultaneous. If there is only a single processor capable of dealing with such brief stimuli, then it can process only one of them. Any capacity for switching attention between stimuli ("timesharing") would be much more useful for the temporally distributed information of quasi-simultaneous digits. Hence performance would be much better than for CVs, particularly under the circumstances used by Springer et al. where the subjects were required to report *both* stimuli. Thus, the "ipsilateral suppression" may only reflect the primary responsibility of each hemisphere to preferentially process the information from the contralateral auditory half-field.

I conclude this overview of the right/left performance asymmetries in dichotic listening experiments by emphasizing that an observed right/left performance asymmetry does not provide *prima facie* evidence that there is hemispheric specialization for the particular type or category of stimuli that was used in the experiment. I have focused on the issue of suppression because it represents a fundamental assumption from which the field of laterality research infers that the right/left asymmetry in *all* dichotic listening experiments derives from hemispheric specialization. With this critical assumption in doubt, the entire inferential chain collapses.

TACHISTOSCOPIC VISUAL EXPERIMENTS

Visual-Spatial Stimuli

I now turn to the subject of tachistoscopic visual studies. I begin with a paper by Hellige (1978), a respected experimentalist in the field of laterality research, who starts his report with the following two sentences: "Material that requires verbal processing typically leads to a right visual field-left hemisphere (RVF-LH) recognition and latency advantage for right-handed adults. In contrast, material which requires nonverbal, visuospatial processing typically leads to either no visual field difference or a left visual field-right hemisphere (LVF-RH) advantage" (p. 121). Hellige then described the results of an experiment on right-handed subjects using three types of stimuli; words, 12-sided polygons of irregular shape, and 16-sided polygons of irregular shape. The last two types of stimuli, illustrated on the left and right sides respectively of Fig. 18, were created by Vanderplas and Garvin (1959). In the first experiment, which he calls the "pure list," the subjects were briefly exposed in separate *blocks* of trials to the words, 12-sided polygons, and 16-sided polygons. In the second experiment the same subjects were exposed to the three types of stimuli in *random* order ("mixed list"). In both cases, only one word or polygon was presented at a time, sometimes in the right visual field other times in the left. After each

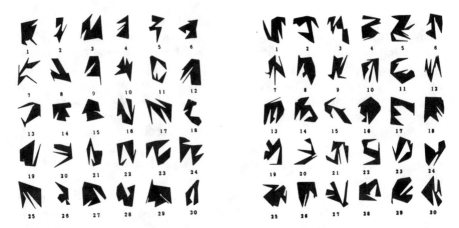

FIGURE 18. Examples of 12- (on left) and 16-sided (on right) irregular polygons created by Vanderplas and Garvin (1959) used by Hellige (1978).

exposure, the subject had either to name the word or pick out the polygon that had been presented from a response card containing 5 polygons with the same number of sides as the stimulus.

The results are shown in Fig. 19. Note first the performance asymmetry in the blocked condition ("pure list" experiment). There is a right visual half-field recognition superiority for words. Although there is no significant field difference for 16-sided polygons, the 12-sided polygons are recognized significantly better in the *left* visual field. When the 12- and 16-sided polygons are presented randomly, however, the results were *doubly reversed*: Now there is no significant right/left recognition asymmetry for the 12-sided polygons, but a highly significant *right* visual field superiority for the 16-sided polygons.

To account for the polygon results in terms of hemispheric specializations, one would be forced to conclude that the *left* hemisphere is specialized for processing 16-sided polygons—but only when presented *randomly* with 12-sided polygons—and that the *right* hemisphere is specialized for processing 12-sided polygons—but only when presented in *blocks* of trials. Such an interpretation strains credulity well beyond the breaking point. I hasten to add that Hellige recognized the absurdity of such a conclusion, at least implicitly, when he explained these results in terms of an interaction among four different factors. In a previous report (Hellige & Cox, 1976), in which 12- and 16-sided polygons were also used, it was concluded that, "The complete pattern of results indicates that several factors including cerebral hemisphere specialization, stimulus codability, selective perceptual orientation, and selective cerebral hemisphere interference interact in systematic ways to produce overall visual laterality effects"

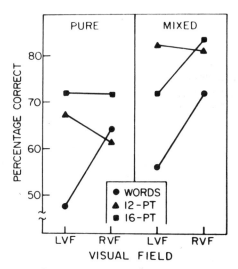

Figure 1. Percentage of correct responses as a function of visual field for the pure-form and pure-word groups (left panel) and for the mixed group (right panel). (The parameter in each panel is type of stimulus: words, 12-point forms [12-PT], and 16-point forms [16-PT]. LVF = left visual field; RVF = right visual field.)

FIGURE 19. Reproduced from Hellige (1978). Visual laterality patterns for pure- versus mixed-list presentation. *Journal of Experimental Psychology: Human Perception and Performance, 4;* 121-131. Copyright 1978 by the American Psychological Association. Reprinted by permission of APA and the author.

(p. 210). Later in this chapter I will show you that this cautiously worded conclusion—which you will note *degrades* the status of hemispheric specialization to only one of four "factors"—deals a devastating blow to the field of laterality research.

Linguistic Stimuli

The "typical" right visual field superiority for the recognition of words (seen in Fig. 19) has been almost universally attributed to the transmission of degraded information from the right hemisphere to the left, where the linguistic material is presumed to be decoded. You will not be surprised to hear that the direction and magnitude of this performance asymmetry also exhibits major individual variation among right-handed subjects—whose left hemispheres are presumed to be specialized for language. Hines,

Fennell, Bowers, and Satz (1980) found test-retest correlations to be extremely low, 0.29. Chiarello, Dronkers, and Hardyck (1984), in a study of right-handed subjects, found that, with words presented to either the right or left half-field, only 62% of subjects exhibited a statistically significant right- or left-field superiority on *either* the test or retest session. Furthermore, 23% of the subjects shifted direction of the field asymmetry on retest. The authors concluded "that the overall statistically significant RVF effect actually reflects the stable performance of less than half (42%) of the subjects" (p. 369). These figures are remarkably similar to those I have already cited in the auditory modality (Speaks et al., 1982). Thus the right visual field performance superiority with tachistoscopically presented words is no more "typical" than the right-ear superiority for words in dichotic listening experiments.

Before I describe the next experiment, I must emphasize that the expectation of a right-field superiority for visually presented linguistic material is rooted in the *anatomical fact* that demonstrable neural connections from retinal elements activated by stimuli in the right visual half-field go to the left striate cortex, and the reverse occurs for stimuli presented in the left visual field. Since the linguistic information sent to the right striate cortex is presumed to have a longer and more arduous route to the left-hemisphere speech centers, laterality theorists anticipate a right half-field advantage.

I now want to describe one of two fascinating and critically important series of experiments by Robertson and Lamb (1988, 1989), both of which demonstrate that this undeniable feature of human anatomy is *not* the key element that determines the performance asymmetry with linguistic material. Figure 20 illustrates their experimental design. It is easier to understand their first experiment if you look first at the two rectangles on the left. Four letters, Rs, are flashed for 100 milliseconds in either the right *or* left visual field, at random, although only the right field condition is illustrated in this figure. Also at random, the cluster of Rs was presented either in their normal orientation or mirror-image reversed as in the lower left rectangle. The subjects were instructed to fixate on a small white light, located at the small "x" in the illustration, until after the exposure of the letters. They were then to indicate, by pressing one of two reaction-time keys, whether the letters were normally oriented or mirror-image reversed. The same subjects also performed two other experiments: The projection slides were re-randomized and then projected on the screen with either a 90° clockwise rotation (+90°) or a 90° counterclockwise rotation (- 90°). Although the subjects were informed prior to each experiment whether they would be observing upright letters, the clockwise or the counterclockwise rotated letters, they were not permitted to tilt their heads, and compliance with this instruction was ensured by monitoring through a one-way mirror.

Figure 21 shows the results. The data are plotted using two abscissae: The

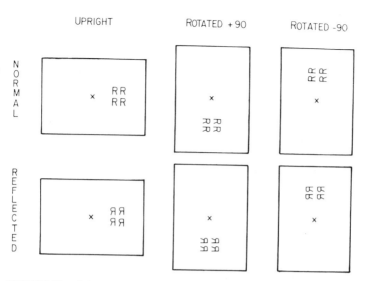

FIGURE 20. Stimuli used by Robertson and Lamb (1988). See text for discussion. Reprinted with permission from *Neuropsychologia, 26;* Robertson, L.C. and Lamb, M. The role of perceptual reference frames in visual field asymmetries, Copyright 1988, Pergamon Press.

FIGURE 21. Results of Robertson and Lamb (1988). The ordinate is reaction time. The abscissa labeled Absolute Location indicates the actual location of the cluster of Rs which could be in the right, left, upper, or lower visual field. The abscissa labeled Relative Location indicates the visual field into which the stimuli would have been projected had the subject been permitted to rotate his head so that the Rs appeared upright. Reprinted with permission from *Neuropsychologia, 26;* Robertson, L.C. and Lamb, M. The role of perceptual reference frames in visual field asymmetries, Copyright 1988, Pergamon Press.

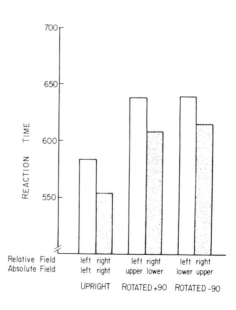

actual locations of the cluster of Rs (called the Absolute Field by Robertson and Lamb) could be in the right, left, upper, or lower visual field. The second abscissa (which they call the Relative Field) represents the visual field in which the stimuli would have been projected had the subjects rotated their heads, or *imagined* that they had rotated their heads (which they *were* encouraged to do). Consider first the results with upright letters. There is a highly significant right visual field superiority in discriminating between normal and mirror-image reversed letters, as indicated by the faster right-field reaction times, a result consistent with most previous reports that letter recognition is superior in the right visual field due to the presumed left-hemispheric specialization for linguistic processing. When the stimuli are rotated 90° clockwise, however, there is a *lower* visual field performance superiority; and when the stimuli are rotated 90° counterclockwise there is an *upper* visual field performance superiority. In brief, the visual field exhibiting the superior performance is in accordance with the *imagined* mental rotation of the display that the subjects were encouraged to perform. This occurs despite the fact that the stimuli in these two rotated conditions were not *anatomically* projected to the right and left hemispheres respectively. The authors concluded, "The direction of asymmetry was predicted not from absolute locations in space determined by the *visual pathway* but from locations *relative* to a selected reference frame" (p. 149).

To put the conclusion slightly more forcefully than Robertson and Lamb do, I would say that their results indicate that it doesn't seem to matter whether information from the stimulus is anatomically projected to the right or left hemisphere. What matters is where the subject *imagines* the stimuli were directed, and anatomy be damned! It is obvious that these results simply cannot be explained in terms of Kimura's direct/indirect access theory—indeed, they reflect a fatal flaw in it.

MULTIPLE FACTORS INFLUENCING RIGHT/LEFT ASYMMETRIES

This review of only a few of the difficulties that arise when one attempts to infer hemispheric specializations from right/left performance asymmetries, in both the visual and auditory modalities, indicates why the more sophisticated researchers in the field of laterality research have recently abandoned the simplistic notion that the *direction* of the observed asymmetry provides *prima facie* evidence of the hemisphere that is specialized for the task. The growing trend, which is well illustrated by Hellige's conclusions about polygons, is to identify various subject and experimental *factors* that contribute to the observed right/left performance asymmetries on a specific task.

Figure 22 contains an abbreviated list of some of the factors that have been discussed. All I have done is to group them into three general and somewhat overlapping categories: subject, stimulus, and methodological variables. The primary purpose of this list is to emphasize that when laterality researchers say that "several factors" are involved in producing laterality effects, they are not talking about just a *few* critical factors but about *many* of them. Each of these modulating variables, moreover, may *increase* the magnitude of an observed right/left performance asymmetry, *decrease* it, or even *reverse* its direction.

Please note the last item in the table: hemispheric specialization for the task. I put it in bold type to emphasize that it is no longer considered to be the *only* source of the asymmetry: Its status has been downgraded to only *one* of four factors in Hellige's explanation of the polygon effects. It thus appears to have lost its exalted status as the only source of right/left asymmetries, not only for Hellige but for other researchers as well.

Like the concept of "glasnost," the introduction of the concept of "modulating factors," and the downgrading of hemispheric specializations to the status of simply another factor that can influence the right/left performance asymmetries, have opened up a closed conceptual system to new ideas. And like glasnost, they have also uncovered problems that had been previously ignored. Once hemispheric specialization is no longer viewed as the *sole* cause of right/left performance asymmetries, even a bright high-school algebra student is likely to ask the awkward question,

FACTORS INFLUENCING R/L ASYMMETRY

SUBJECT	STIMULUS	METHOD
sex	energy	name
age	location	match to sample
handedness	contrast	localize
education	size	detect
language	complexity	reaction time
set	threshold	randomization
strategy	number of	concurrent tasks
practice	difficulty	evoke potential
attention	verbalizability	recognize
imagination	duration	selective report

hemispheric specialization for task

FIGURE 22. List of some of the factors currently believed to have an effect on right/left performance asymmetries in visual and auditory modalities in normal subjects.

"If so many variables can influence an observed performance asymmetry, how can you decide whether a right-ear or right-visual-field performance superiority in a particular task is a result of a *left*-hemispheric specialization or of an 'underlying' *right*-hemispheric specialization that has been *reversed* by one or more of the modulating factors?" To which I will add: "....and how do you know that hemispheric specialization for the task is even *one* of the factors?" Unfortunately, no one in the field of laterality research can answer this question. And what is still worse, no one in the field has formally acknowledged this formidably difficult problem.

To explain why the problem is so difficult I will take the simplest possible case: an experiment in which there are only *two* factors, the presumed hemispheric specialization for the task and a *single* modulating factor. Three pieces of information are then required to answer the student's question. First, you need a *quantitative* measure of the effect and the direction (right or left) of the "underlying" hemispheric specialization factor on the performance asymmetry. Second, you need a *quantitative* measure of the effect and direction of the other factor. Of course, each of these two measures has to be made *independently*. Third, you have to make some testable assumption about the mathematical operation by which the two measures combine to yield the *net* effect. These are the requirements for a *single* modulating factor. For each *additional* factor that might influence the outcome another independent measure of the magnitude and direction of its effect must be provided, as well as an assumption of the mathematical operation by which *its* effects combine with the other factors.

In essence the problem is identical to balancing your checkbook: Deposits indicated by positive values, withdrawals indicated by negative values, and the balance being the algebraic sum of the positive and negative values. Balancing a checkbook is appreciably easier, however, because your banker will accept *only* an algebraic sum! In the field of laterality research it is probably impossible to obtain independent measures of the direction and magnitude of the effect of each factor let alone the combinatorial rules. I need say no more on this issue, except possibly to wish Hellige the best of luck should he undertake the required analysis of his *four* factors so that we can learn which hemisphere (if either) is "really" specialized for recognizing 12- and 16-sided polygons!

You may feel that I have been overly critical of the claim that right/left performance asymmetries arise or are even *related* to hemispheric processing differences. Although I plead guilty to having expressed these negative views somewhat forcefully, I am not alone in my criticisms. Indeed, with much more diplomacy, one member of this audience, Alinda Friedman, in a paper with Martha Polson (Friedman & Polson, 1981), has said

In fact, it could be argued that the most frequent findings to emerge in well over 100 years of research are (a) the apparent capriciousness of the phenomena, that is, the ease with which relatively superficial changes in stimuli, instructions, or other task parameters can switch a performance advantage from one hemisphere to the other; (b) the large amount of data that defy replication across laboratories and paradigms; (c) the wide range of individual performance differences observed on tasks that are supposed to be lateralized one way or another, even among populations suspected to be relatively homogenous in their degree of lateralization of function, such as right-handed males; (d) the lack of consistency within individuals in the degree of lateralization they show across time and tasks; and finally, (e) the absence of a global theory that can adequately explain the factors underlying even the existing regularities that have been observed. (p. 1031)

Well, I have been critical, but not much more so than Professors Friedman and Polson! And I have not yet even *mentioned* the *other* half of the problem that afflicts the field of laterality research. I turn to this problem now.

UPPER/LOWER VISUAL FIELD PERFORMANCE ASYMMETRIES

One unfortunate aspect of the closed conceptual world of hemispheric specializations is that the *only* phenomena considered to be "interesting" are those that relate to the right/left axis of human performance. This continuing conceptual bias is reflected not only in the very name of the discipline — laterality research — but also in the almost studied indifference to reports of performance asymmetries on the vertical axis. Once you know about them, however, it is obvious that a more broadly based and radically different conceptual structure is required to account for *all* asymmetries. To find examples of upper/lower field performance asymmetries, one has to look at visual research conducted by individuals who were *not* concerned with hemispheric specialization of cognitive function, but whose interests lay elsewhere. In the remaining part of this chapter I will describe a few of the experimental results revealing that the right/left asymmetries are often rather puny effects compared to those that have been ignored.

The first of these reports was by M. Mishkin, the sixth MacEachran lecturer, and D.G. Forgays (Mishkin & Forgays, 1952). At the time Mishkin and Forgays did this work they were young graduate students of D.O. Hebb, and neither they nor Hebb were interested in what was then called "cerebral dominance." Rather, they were interested in Hebb's cell-assembly theory of the neurophysiological effects of learning and habits. Their experiment involved presenting common English words for 150 msec, one at a time, randomly in one of four retinal locations: the right, left, upper, or lower visual half-fields. As seen in Fig. 23, correct recognition of the words was twice as high in the right visual half-field compared to the left, and performance in the lower visual half-field was comparably superior to that of the upper visual half-field. Since they were interested in the effects of *learning*, they repeated *part* of this experiment in another group of subjects who were bilingual in English and Hebrew, the latter a language read in the reverse direction. They presented English and Hebrew words *only* in the right and left visual field, but the subject did not know from trial to trial in which visual field or in what language the word would appear. With English words there was, once again, a significantly higher recognition score in the right visual field; but with Hebrew words there was a higher recognition score in the left visual field, albeit not a statistically significant one.

Mishkin and Forgays concluded that their failure to obtain a statistically significant *reversal* of the visual field superiority might have been related to the fact that in all their bilingual subjects, English was the native and more proficient language. This conclusion was buttressed by the fact that the overall performance with English words was superior to that obtained with Hebrew words. A later report by Orbach (1953) substantiated this conclusion in bilingual readers. Using Hebrew and English words, he found that subjects who had learned English as their first language exhibited a *right*-field superiority for Hebrew word recognition, whereas those for whom Hebrew was the first language exhibited an equally significant *left*-field superiority for Hebrew words.

The *point* of the Mishkin and Forgays paper, however, was to show that the right/left asymmetry in word recognition is a consequence of a learned *directional reading habit*, which has nothing whatsoever to do with cerebral dominance for language because right-handed Hebrew-speakers, just like the rest of us, develop aphasia with left fronto-temporal lesions. To

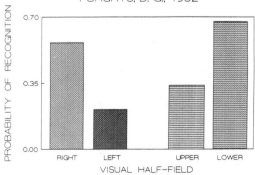

FIGURE 23. Data from Mishkin and Forgays (1952). The ordinate represents the probability of correct word recognition. The abscissa indicates the location of the word. English-reading subjects.

Mishkin's continuing dismay (personal communication), their paper is always cited in the context of discussions of hemispheric specialization for language! As far as I have been able to ascertain, none of the hundreds of investigators over the next 37 years who dutifully cited the Mishkin-Forgays study appears to have thought that the equally robust differences in word recognition between the *upper* and *lower* visual fields in the paper they were citing needed to be mentioned or explained—yet another example of the failure to discuss *divergent* evidence!

The second report is by W. Heron (also a graduate student in Hebb's laboratory) and contained a number of experiments (Heron, 1957). I will describe only one of them, in which Heron used *groups* of four letters arranged in a small square configuration, either in the right *or* left visual field, as illustrated in Fig. 24. Although he found that *overall* letter recognition was superior in the right visual field, he *also* found that *within* both visual fields performance was best for the letter in the upper left corner and decreased monotonically for the upper right, lower left, and lower right corners of the array. This is seen in Fig. 25, which contains Heron's data. These results are of particular interest because they show that the differences in recognition performance *within* a half-field are of *much* greater magnitude than those *between* the two half-fields: The difference in recognition performance between the upper-left corner and the lower-right corner is very large despite the close spatial proximity of these locations, and is about seven times larger than the differences between the two half-fields represented by the separation between the two lines.

Some of the subjects, Heron wrote, "reported that this was the way they saw the letters. That is, it seemed to them that they attended to the letter in the left upper corner first, and the one in the right lower last. This impression was so vivid to some Ss that they said that it felt as if they were

LETTER RECOGNITION AS FUNCTION OF POSITION

HERON, W. (1957) Perception as a function of retinal locus and attention
Amer. J. Psychol, 70; 38–48

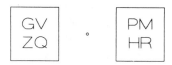

FIGURE 24. Stimuli used by Heron (1957). Four randomly-selected letters arranged in a square configuration. The square was presented either to the left or right of the point of visual fixation. Subjects were required to report all four letters.

DATA FROM W. HERON, 1957

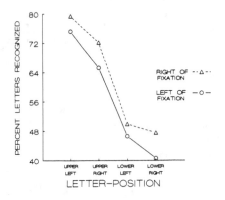

FIGURE 25. Data from Heron (1957). The ordinate represents the percentage of letters reported correctly. The abscissa represents the four locations within the square illustrated in Fig. 24. The values plotted with triangles represent performance when the four letters were in the right visual field; those with circles when the four letters were in the left visual field.

fixating each letter in turn — though this, of course could not occur with the 100 m.sec exposure" (p. 43).

Heron concluded that this pattern of results occurred as a consequence of an *attentional scan* of a post-exposural trace following the brief stimulus, and that the *order* in which the letters within the square was scanned was determined by the directional reading habits of his English-speaking subjects. Although Heron's attentional scanning hypothesis attracted considerable initial interest, it was ultimately dismissed as a manifestation of reporting bias, that is, the order in which the subjects *report* their answers, and not from the order in which the information in these four locations is attentionally scanned. There were only a few, most notably White (1969, 1973), who thought that a post-exposural attentional scan also might be the explanation for the right-visual-field performance superiority with linguistic material, an asymmetry that at the time was being universally attributed to a left-hemispheric specialization for language processing.

Unfortunately, Heron's theory was not seriously pursued until 1983, when Bill Yund and I made another accidental discovery while performing an experiment related to the auditory phenomenon generally referred to as the "cocktail party effect" — the ability to selectively process one acoustic signal in the presence of a number of different and simultaneous sound sources in the auditory field. Previously we had found that the capacity to perform this function was impaired in the auditory half-field contralateral to an anterior temporal lobectomy (Efron & Crandall, 1983; Efron, Crandall, Koss, Divenyi, & Yund, 1983). The lobectomies were designed to minimize the risk of aphasia by making a diagonal incision across the temporal lobe at approximately a 45° angle. This results in a larger removal of the inferior temporal gyrus than the superior temporal gyrus. The work of a number of investigators, the sixth MacEachran lecturer among them, has indicated that the inferior temporal convolution is a visual center. This led us to wonder if the temporal lobectomized patients might also have a deficit in recognizing a familiar object in the *visual* half-field contralateral to their lesion when presented simultaneously with a number of other different objects. Thus we set about creating, as closely as possible, a visual analogue to our cocktail party experiment in the auditory modality. Obviously, we needed neurologically normal control subjects, and it was while we were testing the normals that we stumbled on the unexpected finding (Efron, Yund, & Nichols, 1987).

The experiment we performed is illustrated in Fig. 26, which contains contrast-reversed photographs of the actual sequence of the displays on the computer screen. The subjects were exposed for 133 msec to six different visual-spatial patterns, three on the left and three on the right of the point of visual fixation. After this brief exposure to the patterns, the computer screen was erased and a response card appeared. The subject had to report the box number in which the vertical stripe pattern, the target, had been located. The target was presented randomly in one of the six possible locations, and the locations of the five non-target patterns were also randomized on every trial to counterbalance for any nearby interaction between the target and one or more specific non-target patterns.

We expected that the probability of an error would increase with distance from the fovea; that is, the target would be detected better at locations 3

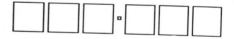

FIGURE 26. Experimental paradigm used by Efron, Yund, and Nichols (1987). For each trial the subject was exposed to six empty boxes seen at the top of the figure. These boxes were then presented again for 133 msec filled with patterns (middle row). Upon termination of this exposure, empty boxes were again displayed with numerals. The subject was required to report the box number in which the vertical stripe target pattern was located, box #2 in the trial illustrated. Contrast-reversed photographs from computer screen.

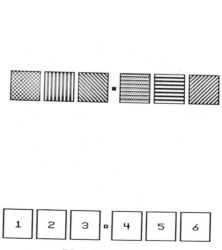

BOX NUMBER ?

and 4 (closest to the fovea) than at locations 2 and 5, where visual acuity is less, and that detection would be poorest at locations 1 and 6. Based on our finding in the *auditory* experiment that normal subjects were right/left symmetrical, we *also* expected that the target would be detected with equal ease at locations *equidistant* from the fovea; that is, performance would be essentially the same for detecting the target at locations 1 and 6, also at locations 2 and 5, also at locations 3 and 4. This expectation of right/left symmetry, however, was not confirmed.

The first few subjects happened to be young males and, as the experimenter entering their responses on the keyboard, I was not aware of any particular pattern of errors. The first female subject, however, seemed to be chronically missing the target when it was in location 3—just to the left of the fovea. I assumed that she had not understood the instructions adequately and so I repeated them. She continued to make mistakes when the target was in location 3. Somewhat frustrated and convinced that she was an idiot, I said to her, "Now look here, you are not paying attention. It is just as easy to see the target in location 3 as in location 4. Come on now, see if you can't do better." She continued to make the same type of error. Those of you who have performed psychophysical experiments on a random selection of subjects know that some of them are absolute duds and, if you are not involved in a population analysis, you drop them from the series. I did just that. I was not aware of any pattern of errors on the next several subjects and then I found another dud, also a female. And yet another and another—again females! By this time, I realized that it was inappropriate for me to eliminate subjects from the experimental series simply because their behavior did not conform to my preconceived ideas, and to atone for this grievous sin I personally ran a rather large number of subjects, 41 males and 41 females, and rejected no further subjects.

Table 2 reveals the mean error rate in the right and left visual half-fields in males and females. It is evident that in the females there is a right-field superiority in the detection of the target, which is highly significant statistically. The males also exhibited a right-field superiority, but this is less marked than in the females and is not statistically significant. You will observe that the performance of females in their right-field is about the same as that of males in either field. The females simply make more errors in the *left*-field than the males.

If you are a true believer in hemispheric specialization, this finding will be disturbing for *two* reasons: First, the *right* hemisphere is widely believed to be specialized for visual-spatial tasks, and this experiment surely is such a task. But if that were true then one would expect a *left* visual half-field superiority, which was not seen in *either* sex group. Second, all true believers know that females are "less lateralized" than males: Their two cerebral hemispheres are believed to be less "specialized" than is the case for

TABLE 2
Target Detection as a Function of Visual Half-Field (Mean Errors)
[Data of Efron, Yund, & Nichols, 1987]

	LEFT VISUAL FIELD	RIGHT VISUAL FIELD	BOTH FIELDS
FEMALES	4.7	2.6	3.7
MALES	2.7	2.3	2.5
BOTH	3.7	2.4	3.1

men. If there were any truth to this idea, which I and others doubt (see Fairweather, 1982), then we obtained the *opposite* result: Females appeared to be *more* "lateralized" than males! If you are a "neurosociologist" or "neuropolitician," an adherent of the new and highly imaginative disciplines I described in Chapter 1, you might be tempted to conclude that because women tend to be more politically conservative than men, they are less inclined to be attracted to the left and thus make more more errors in their left visual fields!

Before accepting such a momentous conclusion, however, it might be a good idea to examine the results more carefully. Table 3 shows the performance of males and females and the sex difference at *each* of the six locations. At first glance, the difference in error rates between males and females at the six locations appears to reveal no underlying pattern, except that it is noticeably more marked in the left visual field, and particularly just to the left of the fovea. But on more careful inspection you will note that the sex difference in error rate in the *right* visual field increases from left-to-right, from locations 4 to 6 respectively. And that in the left visual field the sex difference in error rate *also* increases from left-to-right, from locations 1 to 3 respectively. Indeed, in terms of the *size* of the sex difference the separate sequences in the two visual half-fields actually form a single sequence, 4-5-6-1-2-3, beginning at the location just to the right of the fovea, where there is *no* difference in performance between the sexes, moving rightward in the right visual field, returning to the far left and then again moving rightward within the left visual field back toward the point of fixation.

TABLE 3
Target Detection as a Function of Location (Mean Errors)
[Data of Efron, Yund, & Nichols, 1987]

	TARGET LOCATION BY BOX NUMBER AND FIELD					
	1 (L)	2 (L)	3 (L)	4 (R)	5 (R)	6 (R)
FEMALES	5.6	4.0	4.4	1.2	1.9	4.7
MALES	4.1	2.2	1.9	1.3	1.7	3.9
FEMALES-MALES	1.5	1.8	2.5	− 0.1	0.2	0.8

Figure 27 contains this information in graphic form. We were startled at the linearity of the relationship and immediately saw its potential meaning. The subjects were *scanning* the six patterns in the sequential order 4-5-6-1-2-3, and women, for some as yet unknown reason, were making progressively more errors at each step of the scan than the males. It also was immediately obvious that this scan could not possibly be due to a sequence of eye movements, because the patterns were not on the screen for sufficient time to permit even *one* eye movement. Thus the scan had to have occurred after the stimulus had ended. Unaware of Heron's 1957 paper for several more weeks, we erroneously concluded that we were the first to discover a post-exposural scan. Although his results had been "explained away" as a bias in the order in which the four letters in the square were reported, no such reporting bias could have occurred in our experiment because the subject had to find and report the location of *only one* pattern, the specified target.

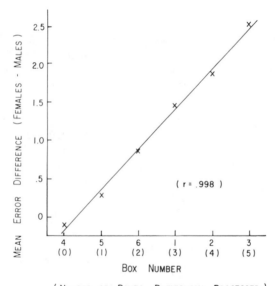

FIGURE 27. Data from Efron, Yund, and Nichols (1987). Ordinate represents the difference in performance (mean errors) between female and male subjects. There are two abscissae: The first indicates the box numbers corresponding to those illustrated in Fig. 26. The second (in parentheses) indicates the number of boxes previously processed and represents the order in which the serial scan examined the six patterns. Reprinted with permission from *Neuropsychologia, 25;* Efron, R., Yund E.W., and Nichols, D.R. Scanning the visual field without eyemovements — A sex difference. Copyright 1987, Pergamon Press. .

I now have to point out why, quite independently, both Heron and we were forced to conclude that the scan had to have occurred *after* the patterns were removed from the screen. If the scan had been so rapid that it was accomplished *while* the patterns were on the screen, there would be no reason for the increase in error rate with each step of the scan. However, if the scan was examining a *decaying* neural representation of the image, then the more time it took to reach the location of the target the more likely it would be that the information at that location would have decayed to a point where the target would be less detectable. Indeed, our remarkably linear result suggests that the decay may be essentially linear, at least for the time necessary to scan the neural representations of six patterns.

There was only one point on which we disagreed with Heron's conclusions: We found no reason to assume that the scan was necessarily *attentional* in nature. In our report (Efron, Yund, & Nichols, 1987), we said

> In using the phrase "non-eyemovement scan" or "scan" we mean only a sequential (serial) mechanism which processes spatially distributed visual information. The phrase contains no implications with respect to the neurophysiological mechanisms which may be used to perform this serial processing, where they may be located in the central nervous system, nor does it imply any particular psychological level (e.g., perceptual or attentional) at which the serial processing occurs. (p. 642)

THE SIGNIFICANCE OF A SCAN

Before describing our subsequent experiments to document the existence of such a scan I want to be sure that you appreciate the *potential* impact that a scanning mechanism might have for the field of cognition. First, it *could* provide a general theoretical framework within which we might better understand at least one of the basic mechanisms by which our central nervous system efficiently deals with the staggering amount of sensory information arriving every second. Put in simple terms, it could explain how we manage to find an object we are looking for visually or auditorily in this absolute avalanche of information. Second, should the scan turn out to be an attentional process, it would markedly enhance our understanding of the properties of attentional processes. Conversely, if it should turn out to be a perceptual process, then it would tell us more about the way sensory systems pre-digest information to be sent onward for subsequent analysis. Finally, in a more restricted context relevant to laterality research, a scan that serially examines the contents of the visual field must necessarily examine some stimuli before others. If there is a tendency to examine stimuli in one visual half-field earlier than those in the other half-field, this would result in a right/left performance asymmetry without involving any hemispheric differences in processing capacity. A scan might thus account for the performance differences *between* the two half-fields and *within* each half-field by a *single* explanation, one that might provide the basis for the global theory called for by Friedman and Polson (1981).

At the very least, the existence of a scan would pose a major new problem for those whose goal is to account for right/left performance asymmetries in terms of hemispheric specializations: In any experiment, the effects of the scan would have to be factored out before any *residual* asymmetry could even be *considered* to arise from differences in hemispheric processing capacity, resources, or styles. In the next chapter I summarize some of our investigations of the scanning mechanism over the past 6 years that indicate how the scanning hypothesis might replace the current explanation for right/left asymmetries in terms of hemispheric specializations.

3

Life After Hemispheric Specialization

INTRODUCTION

By now you must be aware that I am not impressed with the success with which the concept of hemispheric specialization explains right/left performance asymmetries. I have been so diplomatic, however, that you may not have realized that I consider that part of laterality research concerned with performance asymmetries to be *brain dead*. There are a few optimists, it is true, who are engaged in what I believe to be the equivalent of medical heroics. However, since I think they will eventually have to abandon hope and pull the plug on the life-support systems, I will anticipate this outcome and start some thinking about the afterlife. That is why this chapter bears the title "Life After Hemispheric Specialization."

My goal in this chapter is to provide an outline of an alternative explanation for these asymmetries, one not based in any way on the concept of hemispheric specialization, a concept so inherently focused on the right/left axis of performance that it must perforce ignore all other axes on which performance differences occur. The key features of the proposed alternative are: (1) It accounts for the right/left performance asymmetry; (2) It also explains the marked within-field performance differences (described in the previous chapter); and (3) It makes interesting and precise predictions that are experimentally testable, unlike the post-hoc explanations that dominate the existing laterality literature.

THE SCANNING HYPOTHESIS

Three questions are raised by our first experiment (illustrated in Fig. 28). The first is whether we could find evidence for a visual scanning mechanism if the patterns were spatially arranged in a different configuration, one not influenced by the left-to-right habitual reading direction of our subjects. A second issue arises because our results show that performance at the six target positions is determined by *both* the differences of retinal acuity *and* the temporal order in which the six locations were scanned. Would there still be evidence for a scan if we minimized the confounding effect of differences in retinal spatial resolution by placing all the patterns at locations equidistant from the fovea? The third question is raised by the fact that our first experiment required the subjects to localize the target. With such a method, it was at least possible that we were measuring variations in the capacity to *localize* the target as a function of its retinal location, not variations in the accuracy of target *detection* at those locations. Would there be evidence for a scan if the subjects were not required to localize the target?

To answer these questions we performed two experiments (Yund, Efron, & Nichols, 1990a) in which the target and the non-target stimuli were all located at points equidistant from the fovea, in a circular configuration that is unlikely to be influenced by habitual reading direction. The subjects were not required to localize the target, moreover, but only to report whether they saw it or not. In both experiments the target was present on 75% of the trials. When present, it appeared (randomly) in one of twelve locations on a circle equidistant from the point of visual fixation. The two experiments were performed on the same group of 60 right-handed subjects in counterbalanced order. Experiment I used the same type of patterned stimuli and the vertical striped target that were employed in our previous experiment (Efron et al., 1987). Experiment II used a radically different stimulus: a cluster of six omega symbols presented on a background of visual noise, stimuli similar to those used by Julesz (1984) in his experiments on preattentive visual processing. Both experiments are illustrated in Fig. 28. The panels on the left illustrate Experiment I, while those on the right illustrate Experiment II. In both experiments the stimuli were on the screen for only 50 milliseconds to ensure that no eye movements could occur.

Panels A and B in Fig. 29 contain the results of Experiments I and II, respectively. Marked differences in target detectability as a function of retinal location are evident in both experiments. I will refer to each of the 12 possible locations of the target by the numbers 1 through 6 from top to bottom of each half-field, and will refer to the entire *pattern* of detectability differences at the various locations as a "detectability gradient." Our goal is to account for the difference in the *shape* of the detectability gradient between the two experiments.

The results of Experiment II (the cluster of omega symbols) are discussed first because they shed a great deal of light on the results of Experiment I. You can observe in Panel B of Fig. 29 that the cluster of omegas was

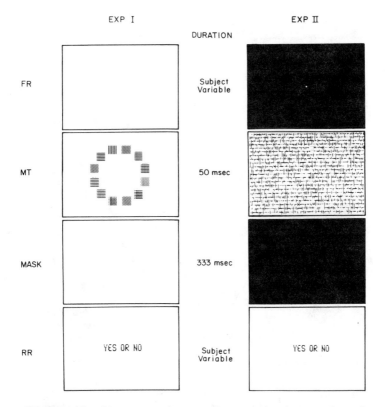

FIGURE 28. Sequence of contrast-reversed photographs of stimuli used in Experiments I & II (Yund, Efron, & Nichols, 1990a). See text for discussion. Reproduced by permission of *Brain and Cognition* and the authors.

detected best at locations 3 and 4 within both visual half-fields, and worst at the top and bottom of each half-field (locations 1 and 6). There also is a weak tendency for the target to be detected better at all locations in the right visual field than in corresponding retinal locations on the left, although these are very small compared to the within-field differences.

The purpose of using a circular configuration of possible target locations was to *minimize* the effects of differences in spatial resolution that were so evident in our previous experiment with stimuli arranged on a horizontal line. It is known that detectability thresholds for all spatial frequencies increase with distance from the fovea, but more markedly in the vertical than in the horizontal direction (Rijsdijk, Kroon, & van der Wildt, 1980). This functional finding is supported by anatomical evidence that cone density also decreases more markedly with increasing distance from the fovea in the vertical than in the horizontal direction (Curcio, Sloan, Packer,

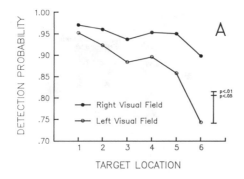

TARGET LOCATION

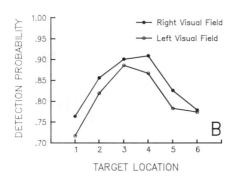

TARGET LOCATION

FIGURE 29. Results of Experiments I & II in Fig. 28 by Yund, Efron, and Nichols (1990a). Panel A contains data for Exp. I while Panel B is for Exp. II. In both panels the abscissa represents the target location numbered from 1 to 6 from top to bottom of the visual half-field. The ordinate is the probability of target detection. Reproduced by permission of *Brain and Cognition* and the authors.

Hendrickson, & Kalina, 1987). The elliptical shape of the gradient for detecting the cluster of omegas seen in Panel B, therefore, is precisely what one would expect on the basis of the known variations in visual resolution at locations on a circle centered on the fovea. I will call this a "resolution" gradient, because its shape is consistent with these differences in retinal resolution.

Now comes the key question: Why is there no indication of this elliptically-shaped resolution gradient in Experiment I (Panel A of Fig. 29)? The vertically striped target, you will recall, had to be detected at the *same* 12 retinal locations as the clusters of omegas. If the target were sufficiently above the threshold for retinal resolution at all locations, there should have been *no* differences in detectability among the 12 locations: The detectability gradient should have been flat. If the target were just above the threshold for retinal resolution, we should have seen at least *some* indication of a resolution gradient. There is none. Instead there is a detectability gradient exhibiting (1) a robust right visual half-field detection superiority, and (2) pronounced differences within each half-field. In both the left as well as the right visual half-fields target detection is highest at location 1 and lowest at location 6. It is evident that the detectability gradient observed in

Experiment I cannot be attributed to the known differences in retinal resolution among the 12 locations, but must arise from a *different* source.

After ruling out alternative explanations for the shape of the detectability gradient in Experiment I, such as artifacts due to our equipment, psychophysical methods, lateral masking effects, long-range retinal interactions, and so forth, we tentatively concluded that the most likely explanation for this detectability gradient is the *temporal order* in which the 12 locations were serially processed by a post-exposural scan of a decaying neural representation of the image. We recognized, of course, that this was "diagnosis by exclusion," and that much more direct and convincing evidence of the existence of a scan would be required. Our next task was to determine more directly whether the detectability gradient of Experiment I was being generated by a serial process (a scan) or a parallel process.

DISTINGUISHING SERIAL FROM PARALLEL PROCESSING

There are two ways by which a computer or a brain can do a job: all of it at once (a parallel process), or one part at a time (a serial process). Of course there is a third way, and that is to do some parts of a complex task all at once and other parts one at a time, but this merely underscores the point that, at root, there are only two ways to do any task — in parallel or serially. Since the brain unquestionably employs both procedures, the cognitive neuroscientist wants to know which tasks are performed serially and which ones are performed in parallel. How does he find out?

Fortunately, there is a commonly used method to make this distinction. Suppose I seat you in front of a wall containing a number of randomly located non-red tiles and ask you to press a key as soon as you detect the single red tile, the target. If you detect the target by a serial processing method, by examining one tile at a time, then it will take you progressively more time to find the red tile if there are 10, 100, or 1000 non-red tiles that you have to examine before you find the red one. The reaction time for detecting the target tile will thus vary *directly* with the number of non-red tiles that are present. However, if the colors of the tiles are processed all at once, in parallel, then the reaction time for detecting the presence of the red tile will not be materially affected by the number of non-red tiles. This principle does not apply only to a reaction time method, of course. An analogous experiment can be performed equally well if the wall of tiles is illuminated briefly with a photographer's flash and the *accuracy* of detection is measured as a function of the number of non-red tiles that are present. The only difference is that with this second method serial processing is indicated by an *inverse* relationship between detectability performance and the number of non-red tiles that must be examined.

The search paradigm used for Experiment I (Fig. 28) fits this example quite nicely. The subject's task was to detect a target, a pattern of vertical stripes (the red tile of the example) in the presence of 11 non-target patterns (the non-red tiles of the example). In Experiment I we did not vary the number of non-target patterns, but tentatively concluded on the basis of indirect evidence that we were dealing with a post-exposural serial scan. If this conclusion is correct, then detectability of the target should *increase* progressively as the number of non-targets is decreased. Figure 30 illustrates the conditions used to test this prediction (Efron, Yund, & Nichols, 1990a).

THE EFFECT OF THE NUMBER OF NON-TARGET PATTERNS

Trials containing 12, 10, 8, 6, or 4 patterns were presented in random order. The *spatial configuration* of the patterns on a trial was random for the 10-, 8-, 6-, and 4-pattern conditions. This randomization of spatial configuration was used to counterbalance for any possible effects on target detectability due to configuration itself or to the location of the target within that configuration. The stimuli remained on the computer screen for only 16 msec to preclude any effects of eye movements. The target was present on only half the trials of each condition; the subject's task was to report whether the target was or was not present on each trial.

The results of this experiment on 100 right-handed normal subjects are indicated in Fig. 31 by the square symbols using the ordinate on the left. Target detectability is expressed in terms of the d' (d prime) measure derived from signal detection theory (McNicol, 1972). Those of you not familiar with this measure need only keep in mind that a d' of 0 represents a complete inability to detect the target, while a d' of 4 represents virtually perfect detection. So, the higher the d', the greater the detectability. It is evident in Fig. 31 that target detection is a decreasing monotonic function of the number of patterns present—just the relationship expected if the target was detected by a serial process.

Actually we had wanted to perform a *single* experiment in which the number of patterns varied between 1 and 12, but this was precluded by a practical problem that will be discussed in a moment. We thus were forced to perform a second experiment on a different group of subjects, this time using random presentations of 4, 3, 2, and 1 patterns. The results of the second experiment also are indicated in Fig. 31 by asterisks and using the ordinate on the right side of the figure. Note that the results of the second

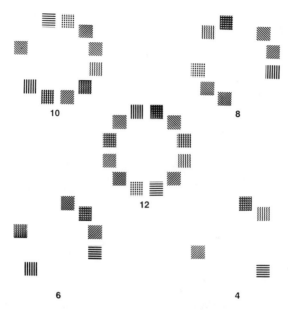

FIGURE 30. Stimuli used by Efron, Yund, and Nichols (1990a). There were five randomly intermixed conditions containing 12, 10, 8, 6, or 4 patterns. The spatial locations of the presented patterns for each condition were selected randomly from the 12 possible locations of the 12-pattern condition. The target was the vertical striped pattern which the subject was required to detect. See Fig. 32, Panel B for the set of 12 non-target patterns used. A second experiment performed on a different group of subjects had four randomly intermixed conditions containing 4, 3, 2, or 1 pattern. See Fig. 32, Panel C for the set of non-target patterns used for the second experiment. See text for discussion. Reproduced by permission of Brain and Cognition and the authors.

experiment are displaced upward on the graph, so that the results of the 4-pattern condition in the two experiments are superimposed.

Although the results of both experiments exhibit the *same* inverse function expected of a serial process, you will notice that overall detectability performance is better in the first than in the second experiment. To explain why this is the case, I first have to explain why we were forced to perform this experiment in two stages. Panel A of Fig. 32 illustrates the set of non-target patterns we intended to use for the 12- to 4-pattern experiment: They were identical to those used in Experiment I of Fig. 28. In pilot experiments using the Panel A non-target patterns, the subjects were so near "ceiling" levels of performance for the 6- and 4-pattern conditions that these two conditions would not have contributed any useful information. Clearly, the experiment had to be made more difficult, and to accomplish this, we were forced to use the non-target patterns illustrated in Panel B of Fig. 32.

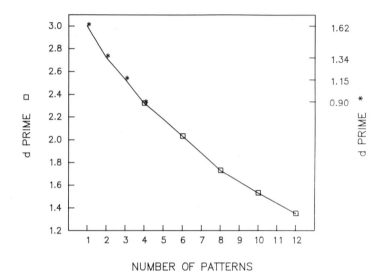

NUMBER OF PATTERNS

FIGURE 31. Results of the two experiments using the set of non-target patterns illustrated in Panels B and C of Fig. 32. The abscissa represents the number of patterns present. The ordinate is the d' measure of target detectability. The results for the 12-, 10-, 8-, 6-, and 4-pattern conditions are plotted with square symbols and use the ordinate on the left; the results of the 4-, 3-, 2-, and 1-pattern conditions are plotted with asterisks and use the ordinate on the right. The data from the 4-, 3-, 2-, and 1-pattern experiment have been displaced upward by an amount sufficient to super-impose the results for the two 4-pattern conditions and to form a single continuous function. Reproduced from Efron, Yund, and Nichols (1990a) by permission of *Brain and Cognition* and the authors.

You will see that some of the non-target patterns in Panel A were replaced with others that had a more marked vertical spatial frequency component. This made the target more difficult to detect and ensured that the subjects would not be at ceiling performance levels within the range from 12 to 4 patterns.

It was imperative, however, for reasons that will become clear shortly, to go all the way down to a 1-pattern condition. Once again, we had the same practical problem when we used the set of non-target patterns in Panel B: Detectabilty was at ceiling levels in the 2- and 1-pattern conditions. Thus for the 4- to 1-pattern experiment we were forced to use the non-target patterns illustrated in Panel C of Fig. 32. You will observe that all four of the non-target patterns used for the 4- to 1-pattern experiment had very marked vertical spatial-frequency components, and with these stimuli the 1-pattern condition was well below ceiling levels of performance. When the results of

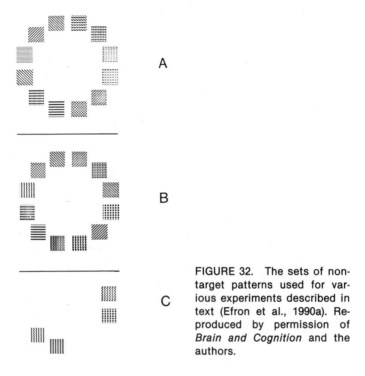

FIGURE 32. The sets of non-target patterns used for various experiments described in text (Efron et al., 1990a). Reproduced by permission of *Brain and Cognition* and the authors.

the second experiment are adjusted on the graph so that the 4-pattern conditions of both experiments are superimposed, as in Fig. 31, you can see clearly that over the entire range of 1 to 12 patterns there is a single monotonic decreasing function.

These results with patterns, coupled with Heron's (1957) experiment with letters described in Chapter 2, leave little doubt that we are dealing with a *serial* processing mechanism, a scan that is examining a decaying neural representation of the visual image. When there are fewer patterns for the scan to search through, there is less time for the information to decay at each location containing a pattern before all of the locations are processed. Thus, overall target detectability decreases systematically as a function of the number of non-target patterns present.

THE ASSUMPTIONS OF THE SCANNING HYPOTHESIS

Before I can describe how we went about studying some of the operating characteristics of this scan, it is essential that I identify, more explicitly than I have so far, the two assumptions of the scanning hypothesis, and their logical implications. The first is that a serial process examines the contents of the entire visual field in *some* temporal order on each trial, an assumption that we can now accept with confidence given the results of the experiments in which the number of non-target patterns was varied. There is no reason, however, to assume that the temporal order in which the stimuli are examined is *identical* on every trial: For example, in a 12-pattern condition there are more than 479 million (12!) different temporal orders in which the stimuli can be sequentially examined. It is exceedingly unlikely that a single subject, let alone a group of subjects, would use the *same* scanning order on every trial with machine-like consistency. On the other hand, if the subjects had used a *different* temporal order on every trial to examine the 12 locations, then over many trials the differences in detectability due to the scan would have been averaged out. Thus there would have been no evidence for a scan, *despite* the fact that one had occurred on every trial. In order to obtain a detectability gradient over many trials of such an experiment, there must be some appreciable *consistency* among the temporal orders in which the locations are examined.

The second assumption of the scanning hypothesis is that the neural representation of the information contained in the brief exposure decays rapidly over time. Since this decay has been the subject of innumerable studies of retinal and central visual persistence for more than 100 years, it hardly needs to be defended. Within the context of the scanning hypothesis it is this decay that produces the differences in detectability as a function of the temporal order in which the stimuli are processed. Thus, the two assumptions, taken together, imply that target detectability decreases as a function of the *elapsed time* before the scan reaches the location occupied by the target.

NUMERICAL MODEL OF THE SCANNING HYPOTHESIS

Although it is easy enough to describe the two assumptions of the scanning hypothesis, it is more difficult to explain how they interact, and how these interactions lead to specific and testable predictions. To facilitate an understanding of the interactive relationship between the assumptions, I will illustrate them in numerical form in a hypothetical experiment in which there are only 8 locations that must be examined serially to find the target. In addition, because we know that there are differences in spatial resolution among different retinal areas, even at locations equidistant from the fovea, these too will be expressed numerically to facilitate understanding of the way in which they would be expected to influence the results of an experiment. This numerical representation of the assumptions is illustrated in Fig. 33.

Please don't panic when you first look at Fig. 33, as it is really not as complicated as it seems initially and merely involves some simple arithmetic. I would normally present such material only in a research report. However, since I have been somewhat arrogant in declaring previous theoretical explanations for performance asymmetries in terms of hemispheric specializations to be bankrupt, I am obliged to convince you of the explanatory power of the proposed alternative, and to do it efficiently.

At the top of the table, the line denoted by "scan order" represents the 8 "steps" of the scan. The left column of the table lists the eight locations that can be considered to be equally spaced in a circle surrounding the fovea. They are designated by the numbers 1 to 4 to indicate their positions from top to bottom in the visual half-field, with the letter R or L to indicate the right or left half-field.

Going back to the top of the table you will see two lines denoted by "Idealized d'." Until I begin to discuss the effects of differences in spatial resolution at the 8 locations, I urge you to ignore the second of these two lines (in which the values are simply seven-tenths of those in the upper line). For the moment we will assume that all 8 locations have the *same* spatial resolution and that it has a nominal value of 1.0 (indicated by the SR = 1.0 in parentheses). This line represents the d' that would be observed if the

MODEL OF SCANNING HYPOTHESIS

Scan Order	1st	2nd	3rd	4th	5th	6th	7th	8th	Example 1		Example 2	
									SR	Observed d'	SR	Observed d'
Idealized d' (SR=1.0)	3.80	3.40	3.00	2.60	2.20	1.80	1.40	1.00				
Idealized d' (SR=0.7)	2.66	2.38	2.10	1.82	1.54	1.26	0.98	0.70				
Location												
1R	.00	.00	.75	.25	.00	.00	.00	.00	1.0	2.900	0.7	2.030
2R	.13	.16	.25	.22	.06	.06	.06	.06	1.0	2.744	1.0	2.744
3R	.13	.16	.00	.00	.71	.00	.00	.00	1.0	2.600	1.0	2.600
4R	.13	.16	.00	.00	.00	.71	.00	.00	1.0	2.316	0.7	1.621
1L	.22	.00	.00	.00	.00	.00	.00	.78	1.0	1.616	0.7	1.131
2L	.13	.17	.00	.00	.00	.00	.70	.00	1.0	2.052	1.0	2.052
3L	.13	.19	.00	.00	.23	.23	.20	.02	1.0	2.360	1.0	2.360
4L	.13	.16	.00	.53	.00	.00	.04	.14	1.0	2.612	0.7	1.828
ALL										2.400		2.046
RVF										2.640		2.249
LVF										2.160		1.843
RVF-LVF										0.480		0.406

Location 1R [SR=1.0] - (0.75 x 3.00) + (0.25 x 2.60) = 2.900
Location 1R [SR=0.7] - (0.75 x 2.10) + (0.25 x 1.82) = 2.030
Location 3R [SR=1.0] - (0.13 x 3.80) + (0.16 x 3.40) + (0.71 x 2.20) = 2.600

FIGURE 33. Numerical representation of assumptions of the scanning hypothesis for a hypothetical 8-pattern experiment. See text for discussion. Reproduced from Efron, Yund, and Nichols (1990a) by permission of *Brain and Cognition* and the authors.

scanning order were *identical* on every trial, complete scanning consistency. As you can see, the spatial location *always* examined on the first step of the scan would have a d' of 3.8, almost perfect detection, the location *always* examined on the second step of the scan would have a lower d' because the information has decayed somewhat, and I have arbitrarily said that it is 3.4, and so on. The only constraint, imposed by the assumption of information decay, is that these idealized d' values, whatever they actually may be for the patterns and target used in a specific experiment, must decrease monotonically. To simplify this presentation, however, I have illustrated a linear decrease. Similarly, I have used a d' measure of target detectability only because the results of the previous experiment were expressed that way: Any other measure of detectability, such as probability of correct report, could have been used equally well.

The large rectangular box contains the *probability* over many trials that each spatial location was "examined" at each step of the scanning sequence. The values for the probability distribution of this hypothetical experiment were arbitrarily selected to illustrate several points that I will explain in a moment. Assuming that each location is examined once and only once on each trial, the constraint on this probability distribution is that the sum of the probabilities across each row and down each column must be 1.0. If the multiple scans were completely *inconsistent* — if on every trial the locations were examined in a *random* temporal order — then every one of the 64 values in this probability distribution would be 0.125. Conversely, if the multiple scans were completely *consistent* — if on every trial the locations were examined in the *same* temporal order — then each row and column would contain a single entry of 1.0. The probability distribution illustrated in Fig. 33 lies between these two extreme conditions: The multiple scans are neither completely consistent nor completely inconsistent. In this hypothetical probability distribution you can see that location 1R was examined on the 3rd step of the scan on 75% of the trials, while it was examined on the 4th step on 25% of the trials; Location 1L was examined on the first step of the scan on 22% of the trials and was examined on the eighth step of the scan on 78% of the trials; and so forth. This probability distribution as well as the idealized d' sections of the table are enclosed in a box to emphasize that they are internal variables whose values, whatever they may be, are not directly observable.

The only information available to the experimenter is the d' value actually measured at each location after many trials, the "observed d'" values in the column under Example 1. For the moment pay no attention to the observed d' values for Example 2. The observed d' values for target detectability in Example 1 are computed simply as the sum of the probabilities for that location multiplied by the idealized d' value corresponding to the appropriate "step" of the scan and the appropriate spatial resolution for that location. Let me show you how it works for location 1R that is scanned third with a probability of 0.75 and fourth with a probability of 0.25. The calculation for the observed d' for location 1R is on the *first* line below the body of the table, 2.900. If location 1R had been on a region of retina with *lower* spatial resolution, one having a nominal value of 0.7, then you would use the "Idealized d' (SR = 0.7)" set of values at the top of the table to calculate the observed d' for this location (illustrated by the calculation on the *second* line below the table). The calculation for the observed d' for location 3R, which is examined on the 1st, 2nd, and 5th steps of the scan is seen on the third line below the table and would be 2.600 if it is at a retinal area with a spatial resolution of 1.0. As I said, it is just simple arithmetic!

Now turn to Example 2 on the extreme right side of the table, which shows how variations in the retinal spatial resolution at the various locations can be incorporated into the model. In this example we assume that the spatial resolution (SR) at retinal locations 1R, 4R, 1L, and 4L is 0.7, but remains 1.0 at the other four retinal locations. The computation of the observed d' for *each* of the locations having an SR = 1.0 uses the "Idealized d' (SR = 1.0)" values at the top of the table while the computation for *each* of the the locations having an SR = 0.7 uses the "Idealized d' (SR = 0.7)" values of the next line. I repeat, it is just simple arithmetic!

PREDICTIONS OF THE SCANNING HYPOTHESIS

The numerical representation of the assumptions underlying the scanning hypothesis in Fig. 33 has *no* predictive value in itself, of course, since the outcome of any experiment can be explained by a post-hoc choice of values for the internal variables: There are so many unknowns that the model could be made to fit virtually any result. The value of such a model, however, is the insight it provides into the interactions between the assumptions of any serial processing mechanism that examines decaying information at multiple locations. With these interactions in mind, one can then design experiments in which the effect of changing certain stimulus parameters *can* be predicted. I now discuss some of these predictions, making repeated reference to Fig. 33.

I begin with the observation that the detectability gradient, the 8 observed d' values, is a reflection of a *probabilistic* tendency for some locations to be examined earlier than others across many trials in a single subject or a group of subjects. In Fig. 33 the values in the probability matrix were selected arbitrarily to simulate a gradient in which there is a right half-field detection superiority with decreasing detectabilities within the right visual half-field from the upper (location 1R) to the lower (location 4R) half of the field, and a gradient in the reverse direction within the left visual half-field. By changing the values within the probability matrix you can simulate any gradient you want, provided you keep the sums of probabilities across rows and across columns at 1.0. Whatever numbers you choose, however, overall target detectability will have a d' equal to the *mean* of the 8 idealized d' values if the spatial resolution at all locations is the same: In Example 1 of Fig. 33, where this condition is fulfilled, it is 2.40 (the line denoted by "All").

This means that any tendency of the scan to examine one or more locations earlier than others will cause target detection at these locations to be higher than that of the others. The *assumptions* of the scanning hypothesis itself, it should be emphasized, are inherently symmetrical. But a right/left and/or an upper/lower half-field performance asymmetry will arise if the probabilistic scanning order examines stimuli in one half-field earlier than those in the other. The probabilistic scanning order that may be used in an experiment is only *one* of the scanning mechanism's operating characteristics to be described in this Chapter. I remind you that all the experiments already described have shown a right-field detection superiority, from which we have tentatively concluded that the scan tends to examine stimuli in the right field earlier than those in the left. Further evidence supporting this conclusion is provided later.

The numerical representation of the two assumptions in Fig. 33 makes it easy to see why overall target detection will improve when the number of non-target patterns is decreased. Figure 33 illustrates the use of 8 patterns. But now imagine that I have reduced the number of patterns presented to 4, and that these 4 patterns can be in any of the 8 locations. Figure 34 illustrates this condition. When a pattern is present at a retinal location, it will always be examined on one of the first four scan steps, and for this reason the probability distribution is left blank for scan steps later than 4. Once again, the sum of the first *four* probabilities across each *row* must be equal to 1.0. The sum of the columns, however, is slightly more complex: The constraint on the sum of the probabilities in each of the four columns must be adjusted for the fact that only 4 of the 8 possible locations contain patterns on any trial and therefore the sum of each column must be 1.0 per 4 locations or 2 times 1.0 in this particular case. So mentally insert *any* set of numbers you want in the four columns on the left but keep the sum of each of the eight rows equal to 1.0 and the sum of each of the four columns equal to 2.0, as illustrated in the table. If you are faster at arithmetic than I am, you will see immediately that whatever numbers you choose, the overall d' *must* increase compared to the condition (Fig. 33) in which there are eight patterns present on every trial. Actually, you need only look at the upper box for this calculation. Because the overall d' must equal the mean of the idealized d' values for the number of scan steps, it changes from 2.40 in Example 1 of Fig. 33 (the mean of all *eight* idealized d' values) to 3.20 in

MODEL OF SCANNING HYPOTHESIS

Scan Order	1st	2nd	3rd	4th	5th	6th	7th	8th	Example 1		Example 2	
									SR	Observed d'	SR	Observed d'
Idealized d' (SR=1.0)	3.80	3.40	3.00	2.60	2.20	1.80	1.40	1.00				
Idealized d' (SR=0.7)	2.66	2.38	2.10	1.82	1.54	1.26	0.98	0.70				
Location												
1R	.40	.30	.20	.10					1.0	3.400	0.7	2.380
2R	.40	.30	.15	.15					1.0	3.380	1.0	3.380
3R	.18	.30	.50	.02					1.0	3.256	1.0	3.256
4R	.10	.00	.65	.25					1.0	2.980	0.7	2.086
1L	.20	.50	.30	.00					1.0	3.360	0.7	2.352
2L	.40	.20	.00	.40					1.0	3.240	1.0	3.240
3L	.19	.25	.10	.46					1.0	3.068	1.0	3.068
4L	.13	.15	.10	.62					1.0	2.916	0.7	2.041
ALL										3.200		2.725
RVF										3.254		2.775
LVF										3.146		2.675
RVF-LVF										0.108		0.100

FIGURE 34. Numerical representation of assumptions of the scanning hypothesis for a hypothetical 4-pattern experiment. See text for discussion.

Example 1 of Fig. 34 (the mean of the *first four* idealized d' values). This is why there is a decreasing relationship between the *overall* level of target detection and the number of non-target patterns that have to be examined to find the target.

It is obvious that a location that was often examined on the 12th step of the scan of 12 patterns could *never* be examined later than the 4th step of the scan if there are only 4 patterns to be examined. This leads to an interesting prediction: Target detection at locations exhibiting *lower* detectabilities in the 12-pattern condition (because they were examined toward the end of the scans) is likely to exhibit a relatively more marked increase in detectability when the number of patterns is decreased than would be the case at those locations having the *higher* detectabilities in the 12-pattern condition. This prediction is confirmed by examining the results of the experiment in which the number of non-target patterns was varied. The results for the 12- to 4-patterns experiment are illustrated in Fig. 35. For example, at locations 3R and 3L, where detection is lowest in the 12-pattern condition, the performance there increases markedly in the 4-pattern condition. At locations 5R and 6R, which have the highest detectabilities in the 12-pattern condition, the increase of detectability in the 4-pattern condition is appreciably less marked. Thus, even without knowing anything about the probabilistic temporal order in which the locations are scanned or the actual values for the idealized d' (the unknown values within the two rectangles in Figs. 33 and 34), the interactions between the two assumptions of the scanning hypothesis lead to a prediction that is confirmed.

The assumptions of the scanning hypothesis also predict that the target is likely to be detected more readily with decreasing number of patterns to be examined, *no matter where it is located*, because it will be processed earlier in the scan as the total number of items that require processing is decreased. The results of the experiment where the number of patterns present varied from 12 to 4 (Fig. 35) confirm this second prediction: There is a monotonic increase in target detection at *every one* of the twelve locations as the number of patterns decreases.

The interaction between the two assumptions of the scanning hypothesis also leads to a third prediction that is of particular importance to the field of laterality research. If the right visual half-field superiority in these

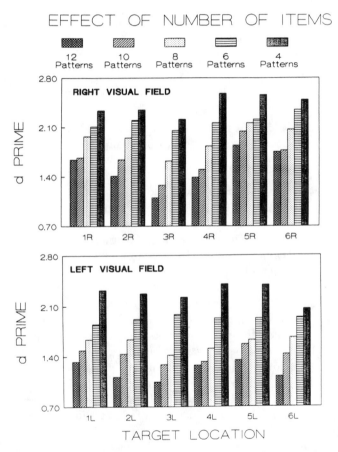

FIGURE 35.   Target detectability at the six right-field locations (upper panel) and the six left-field locations (lower panel) for the 12-, 10-, 8-, 6-, and 4-pattern conditions illustrated in Fig. 30. Data from Efron, Yund, and Nichols (1990a). See text for discussion.

experiments is due to a probabilistic scanning order that tends to examine right-field stimuli earlier than left-field ones, then the right half-field detection superiority should decrease as the number of patterns is decreased, and should disappear entirely in the 1-pattern condition. With only one stimulus to be scanned there *could be no effect of scanning order*: It would always be examined "first." You may recall that earlier I said it was imperative to use a 1-pattern condition in the experiment I have just described. You now know that the results obtained in this condition represent a critical test of the hypothesis that the right-field detection superiority observed in all these experiments reflects an operating characteristic of the scan to examine right-field stimuli earlier than those in the left field. You must also suspect that I would not be spending the time on this point if the results were *not* in accordance with this prediction! Figure 36 shows that this prediction is confirmed. Indeed, the right half-field detection superiority completely disappeared in the 1-pattern condition: There is in fact a trivial (statistically insignificant) *left*-field superiority!

This result is entailed in the two assumptions of the scanning hypothesis: If the number of patterns is progressively reduced, even though the scan tends to go right first, there will be *fewer* patterns in the right field for it to process before it begins to examine those in the left field. Since the scan consumes less time processing the smaller number of patterns in the right

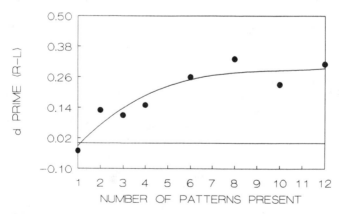

RIGHT–LEFT ASYMMETRY AS FUNCTION OF THE NUMBER OF PATTERNS PRESENT

FIGURE 36. The effect on the right-field detection superiority of reducing the number of patterns. The abscissa is the number of patterns present on a trial. The ordinate represents the d' difference between the two visual fields (right minus left). The curve is a third order polynomial fit to the data. Data from Efron, Yund, and Nichols (1990a). See text for discussion.

field, when it does begin to examine the stimuli in the left field the information in the left half-field will have had less time to decay. Consequently, left half-field target detection will be less impaired than would have been the case if the right field had contained *more* patterns that needed to be examined. The 1-pattern condition is special only in that it represents the extreme limit of this progressive effect. Thus the two assumptions of the scanning hypothesis also predict that if the right/left asymmetry is a result of the probabilistic scanning order, then it must decrease and ultimately disappear as the number of stimuli to be examined is decreased, provided that the stimuli are placed in retinal areas of similar spatial resolution. That this is exactly what occurred provides strong empirical evidence that *any* field superiority—right, left, upper, or lower—derives from the probabilistic order in which the stimuli are examined by this serial processing mechanism.

The prediction that the right/left asymmetry will diminish with decreasing number of non-target patterns, however, must be considered in the context of two claims repeatedly found in the laterality literature. The first is that right/left performance asymmetries are often less marked and may disappear when a task is made too easy. Thus it might be argued that the decrease, and ultimate loss of the right-field detection superiority when the number of patterns was reduced to one may have occurred simply because the task became too easy. This argument is easily refuted: The experiment using the 4-, 3-, 2-, and 1-pattern conditions employed non-target patterns that were very difficult to discriminate from the target. As can be seen in Fig. 31, even in the 1-pattern condition, the d' is much lower (1.62) than that of the 4-pattern condition of the experiment using 12 to 4 patterns where the d' is 2.32. Thus the progressive loss of the right-field detection superiority as the number of patterns decreases from 4 to 1 cannot be due to the fact that the task became too easy.

The second claim often made in the laterality literature is that the degree of *verbal encoding* of the stimuli is an important factor in producing a right field detection superiority, because such verbal encoding makes it more likely that they will be processed in the left hemisphere, which is "specialized" for linguistic activities. However, even if we assume that the right-field detection superiority occurs in the 12-pattern condition because subjects encode the target verbally, say as "jail bars," then why should it progressively decrease and ultimately disappear entirely in the 1-pattern condition, when the target is still being encoded verbally in the same way?

In sum, there are compelling reasons to reject both of these explanations for the loss of the performance asymmetry and to accept the conclusion that the right-field superiority arises from the probabilistic tendency to scan locations in the right field earlier than those in the left. Although I provide further evidence for this conclusion later in this chapter, I want to continue with implications of the two assumptions of the scanning hypothesis.

Inspection of Fig. 33 also reveals that the two assumptions of the scanning hypothesis entail a *reciprocity relationship*: If one or more locations anywhere are examined earlier than the others, then detectability at these locations will be higher, but at the expense of lower detectabilities distributed among the other locations. This follows from the fact that the sum of the probabilities in each row and column of the matrix is 1.0: If one probability increases, one or more *must* decrease. In Chapter 2 I referred to dichotic listening experiments, both in normal and split-brain subjects, in which various manipulations that increased recognition of words presented to one ear did so at the expense of performance in the other ear, but that the total number of words correctly reported from both ears was *constant*. The existence of such a reciprocity relationship in dichotic listening experiments raises the possibility that multiple, spatially separated, *sound* images might also be scanned serially by an analogous mechanism in the auditory system.

Under normal living conditions we are surrounded by multiple simultaneous sound sources: the telephone, air conditioner, people talking at cocktail parties, glasses clinking, people coughing, horns honking, and so forth. One of the tasks we must perform is to find, and then selectively attend, the sound source of particular relevance to our need at that time — at a cocktail party this is often a salacious bit of gossip about one of our colleagues! — and to do so at the expense of not hearing another sound source as well as we might. In this context, it is of considerable interest to note that a paper by Hublet, Morais, and Bertelson (1977) and a more extensive review of the subject by Morais (1978) have described a complex gradient in the accuracy of detecting a target speech sound as a function of its location in the auditory field: Target detection was superior in the right compared to the left auditory half-field and in the auditory field in front of the subject compared to the field behind his head. These findings in the auditory modality provide absolute proof that my mother was right when she warned me, "When I'm talking to you, you'd better look at me!" and "You never know what people are saying behind your back."

More seriously, they raise the possibility that we may be scanning our auditory field in a manner similar to that with which we scan our visual field. If this is the case, then some of the basic assumptions of the visual scanning hypothesis might apply to auditory processing, including the reciprocity relationship and a tendency to scan sound sources in the right-auditory half-field earlier than those in the left. Under conditions in which two sound sources are present at the same time — the typical dichotic listening paradigm — an auditory scan tending to go right first might provide an alternative explanation for the disproportionately large number of right-field performance superiorities in the auditory modality.

The next point illustrated in Fig. 33 is that target detectability, and the resulting shape of the detectability gradient, is determined not only by the temporal order in which the stimuli are scanned, but *also* by differences in retinal sensitivity at these locations. If you compare the observed d' values in Example 1 (where spatial resolution at all locations is identical) with that of Example 2 (where resolution is lower at locations 1R, 4R, 1L, and 4L), you will see that the *shape* of the detectability gradient has changed: In Example 1 there is a monotonic decrease of detectability in the right half-field from 2.900 at location 1R to 2.316 at location 4R, and a monotonic increase in the left half-field from 1.616 at location 1L to 2.612 at location 4L. In Example 2 detectability in both half-fields is superior at locations 3 and 4. The detectability gradient of Example 2 now exhibits the elliptically shaped "resolution gradient" (see Fig. 29, Panel B), *despite* the fact that the probability distribution has not changed.

The elliptically shaped "resolution gradient" seen in Example 2 of Fig. 33 was obtained because of the lower spatial resolution at locations 1R, 4R, 1L, and 4L. It is important to emphasize that a similar shape also will be obtained if we change the set of non-target patterns so that they have more marked vertical spatial frequency components, making the discrimination of the vertical striped target more difficult. In this case, we have not actually *changed* the spatial resolution at these locations, but simply performed the experiment closer to the known differences of spatial resolution threshold at these locations. You may recall in the discussion of the experiment illustrated in Fig. 30 that we were required to make the set of non-target patterns used for the 4- to 1-pattern experiment appreciably more difficult than that used for the 12- to 4-pattern experiment by using non-target patterns with more marked vertical spatial frequency components (Fig.32, Panel C). Consequently, the detectability gradients for the 4- to 1-pattern experiment should exhibit the elliptical shape of a "resolution gradient" in contrast to the 12- to 4-pattern experiment. This prediction is clearly confirmed by the data (see Fig. 3 in Efron, Yund, & Nichols, 1990a and Fig.2 in Yund, Efron, & Nichols, 1990b).

I have now described a sufficient number of the interactions between the assumptions of the scanning hypothesis that you should have some sense of the scope of the predictions it makes. There are other predictions that can be found in our papers on this subject (Efron et al., 1990a; Yund et al., 1990b). You may wonder, however, if we have created a theory that is applicable only to a *restricted* set of stimuli, the grid patterns used in computers to fill in bar charts. We haven't. In the first place it clearly applies to Heron's experiment with letters arranged in a small square. Second, we have tested the generality of the scanning hypothesis with other visual stimuli. Figures 37 and 38 illustrate some of the stimuli we have used: The first, Fig. 37, employed various shapes having both vertical and horizontal spatial frequency components, and the target was the vertical bar. There was a marked right-field detection superiority. The second, Fig. 38, used clusters of symbols, and the target was the cluster of omegas. A

FIGURE 37. Experiment in which a single vertical bar target is presented with non-target stimuli having both a vertical- and a horizontal-bar component. See text for discussion.

strong right-field detection superiority was present. We also used 12 squares of red and blue colors of different brightness (presented at the same retinal loci as the stimuli illustrated in Fig. 37) and the target was a purple square, a color produced by the mixture of red and blue. Once again we observed a strong right-field detection superiority. In sum, regardless of the nature of the stimuli we used, a right half-field detection superiority and a detectability gradient were obtained, indicating that in all three cases we are dealing with a serial scan and that there is nothing unique about the patterns we used initially.

It is of some interest to note that in the several dozen experiments we have performed on large groups of subjects in the context of the scanning hypothesis, we have not observed a single instance of a statistically significant *left*-field detection superiority. A number of writers have commented on the curious fact that the laterality literature contains vastly more reports of right-field superiorities than left-field ones, and that the latter are the ones that are more frequently *not* confirmed. A scanning mechanism that has a probabilistic tendency to examine the contents of the

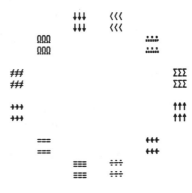

FIGURE 38. Experiment in which the target cluster of four omegas is presented with non-target clusters of other symbols that do not have any curved components. See Julesz (1984) for discussion of texton theory of preattentive vision.

right field earlier than the left might be the explanation for this over-whelming preponderance of reported right-field superiorities. I cannot emphasize too strongly, however, that the assumptions of the scanning hypothesis are symmetrical and do not in themselves predict whether there will be a right, left, upper, or lower field detection superiority in any experiment. We used stimuli other than patterns in the hope that we would find a type of stimulus in which the scan's operating characteristics would give rise to a statistically significant *left*-field superiority in a large group of subjects. Although we have not had any luck in this respect so far, the assumptions of the scanning hypothesis do not preclude this possibility.

In this context it should be mentioned that in all of our experiments in which a right half-field detection superiority was observed for large groups of subjects, we have also found that about 25% of the group exhibit a left-field superiority. Such "aberrant" subjects, of course, pose no problem for the scanning hypothesis since it is not based on any assumption of a right/left asymmetry, unlike Kimura's direct/indirect access theory.

ONE SCANNER OR TWO?

A serial processing mechanism—a scan that examines the stimuli in the *entire* visual field but tends to examine stimuli in the right field earlier than those in the left—represents a radical departure from the prevailing approach that accounts for right-field performance superiorities in terms of a left-hemispheric processing "specialization" for the type of stimuli used. The two approaches appear to be irreconcilable. There is one possible way of trying to reconcile them: Imagine that there are *two* independent scanning mechanisms, one in each hemisphere, each processing only the stimuli in the contralateral half-field. If these two scanning mechanisms have slightly different operating characteristics (e.g., different scanning speeds or different probabilistic scanning orders), this might explain not only why we have consistently observed a right-field detection superiority, but also why we have consistently found differences in the *shape* of the detectability gradients between the right and left half-fields. The differences in the operating characteristics of the two scanners, then, would be just another manifestation of hemispheric differences—and then everyone would be happy!

This benevolent attempt to negotiate a compromise, and to avoid conflict, led us to design an experiment to distinguish between a single scanner hypothesis and a dual scanner hypothesis with a scanner in each hemisphere. The experiment (Yund, Efron, & Nichols, 1990c), illustrated in Fig. 39, utilized three randomly presented conditions: an arc of six patterns either in the right or in the left visual field (Conditions A and B, respectively), and a complete circle of 12 patterns (Condition C). The *dual* serial scanner hypothesis assumes that the detectability gradient in each half-field arises as a consequence of the serial order in which the six patterns in that half- field are examined by its scanner. This hypothesis predicts that the *shape* of the detectability gradient in each half-field, as well as the overall level of target detection there, will be independent of the presence or absence of non-target patterns in the opposite half-field. From its point of view, each of the two scanners "sees" and serially processes only its half of the circle of 12 patterns and therefore would be expected to perform in exactly the same manner whether or not patterns are present in the other half-field.

The *single* scanner hypothesis, however, makes an entirely different prediction: If the scanner tends to examine stimuli in the right field *before* those in the left, as our previous results indicate, then target detection in the solitary right arc (Condition A) and the right half of the circle (Condition C) would not be expected to differ much, because the stimuli in the left half

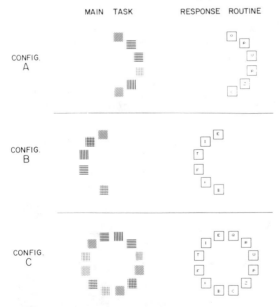

FIGURE 39. Stimuli used by Yund, Efron, and Nichols (1990c). On the left side of the figure are the three randomly intermixed conditions which were presented for 50 msec. After the exposure was terminated, the appropriate response card for that spatial configuration appeared on the screen (illustrated to the right of each configuration of patterns). The subject was required to indicate, by entering a letter on the keyboard, the location of the target. See text for results. Reproduced by permission of *Brain and Cognition* and the authors.

of the circle are largely irrelevant while it is examining the right field. It will get around to examining the stimuli in the left half of the circle only *after* it has consumed time examining some number of right-field stimuli. This time loss, however, will cause the overall detection performance in the *left* side of the *circle* (Condition C) to be appreciably worse than in the case when there are *no* stimuli in the right field that consume processing time (Condition B).

This experiment not only has the capacity to distinguish between the one- and two-scanner hypotheses, but it also serves as another way to test our previous conclusion that there is a tendency for the (single) scanner to go to the right first. The results are unequivocal, both with respect to the *overall* detectability and to the *shape* of the detectability gradients. The data on the overall detectability levels are shown in Fig. 40. It is evident that performance for the solitary right arc is slightly superior than that for the solitary left arc. However, the right/left asymmetry is much more marked in the two halves of the circle, as predicted by the *single* scanner hypothesis. In contrast, the dual scanner hypothesis predicts that there will be *no change* in the right/left asymmetry between the arc and circle conditions, since each scanner only "sees" and processes the same six stimuli whether or not there are any stimuli in the opposite half-field. That prediction obviously is not confirmed.

The results with respect to the *shape* of the detectability gradients are equally unambiguous. As predicted by *both* the single and dual scanning hypotheses, the shape of the detectability gradient for the six locations in the solitary *right* arc is essentially identical to that obtained for the six locations in the right half of the circle, as evidenced by a correlation coefficient of 0.942. The dual scanner hypothesis also predicts that the

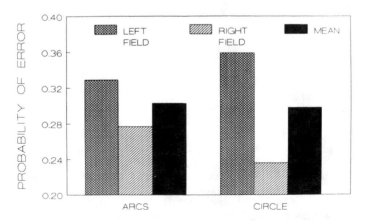

FIGURE 40.   Results of experiment illustrated in Fig. 39. See text for discussion.

shape of the detectability gradient for the six locations in the solitary *left* arc will be essentially the same as that of the left half of the circle, but this is not the case: The two gradients are markedly different, as indicated by a correlation coefficient of only 0.265. The complete pattern of results—with similar gradients for the stimuli in the right half-field and dissimilar gradients for those in the left half-field—is fully in accord with the predictions of the single scanner hypothesis.

In sum, the results of this experiment force us to reject the dual scanning hypothesis and also to reject the possible reconciliation between the way the scanning hypothesis and the concept of hemispheric processing differences account for the right-field detection superiority. Further, they provide additional evidence that one of the operating characteristics of the scan is the tendency to examine stimuli in the right half-field before those in the left. Thus we are dealing with a single scanning mechanism that accesses information from the *entire* visual field; this in turn suggests that the mechanism must be in some part of the visual system beyond the striate cortex, that is, one which possesses interhemispheric connections.

All the experiments I have described so far were performed on right-handed subjects so that any possible effects of the subjects' handedness would not confound the results. But because there are many reports in the laterality literature of differences between right- and left-handed subjects, we wondered whether there also might be differences in the scanning behavior of right- and left-handers. For this reason, the experiment illustrated in Fig. 39 was repeated in a group of 60 left-handed subjects, all of whom had a mother, father, or full sibling who was also left-handed. There were no statistically significant differences between the right- and left-handers. There also were no statistically significant differences between those left-handers who performed *all* unimanual activities with the left hand and those who performed some with the right hand. Our failure to find any difference between right- and left-handed subjects indicates that the shape of the detectability gradients, and thus the probabilistic scan paths, are not related to any genetically determined hemispheric differences that might be associated with handedness or to any acquired functional differences based on preferred hand usage.

OPERATING CHARACTERISTICS OF THE SCAN

The Tendency to Examine Right- Before Left-Field Stimuli

I will now summarize the evidence that the scan has a probabilistic tendency to examine stimuli in the right half-field earlier than those in the left: (1) A right-field detection superiority and even more marked within-field detection differences have been consistently found with pattern stimuli (see Figs. 26, 27, and 28); (2) A right-field superiority and marked within-field differences in detectability are also observed for other types of stimuli, for example, shapes (Fig. 37), clusters of symbols (Fig. 38), colors, and, of course, the letters used by Heron (1957); (3) This right-field superiority diminishes and ultimately disappears when the number of patterns is reduced (see Fig. 36); and (4) The right-field superiority is enhanced for a circle of patterns compared to solitary arcs of patterns in the right or left fields (see Fig. 40).

If the scanning hypothesis is to emerge as a viable alternative explanation for performance asymmetries, then it also must account for *other* aspects of the right-field superiorities that have been attributed to hemispheric differences. I will describe one of these phenomena reported in experiments using *linguistic* material—experiments in which a right half-field superiority is frequently obtained. This right-field superiority with words or letters is appreciably larger when the stimuli are presented in *both* visual fields simultaneously in a single trial (called a "bilateral presentation" mode) than when the stimuli are restricted to a half-field ("unilateral presentation" mode) and the performance in the two half-fields subsequently compared (Hines, 1975; Hines, 1976; Kershner & Gwan-Rong Jeng, 1972; McKeever, 1971; McKeever & Huling, 1971).

These findings have been explained in terms of Kimura's direct/indirect access theory. The explanation goes as follows: Linguistic information presented to the right half-field is assumed to reach a language center in the left hemisphere with greater "signal fidelity" than identical information presented to the left field that reaches this center only indirectly and in a degraded form after transfer via the corpus callosum. The degradation is assumed to account for the weak right-field performance superiority in unilateral presentations. In bilateral presentations, however, the degraded information from the right hemisphere must "compete" for processing with higher fidelity information going directly to the left hemisphere. The failure to compete successfully produces a more marked right-field superiority.

This explanation, of course, rests on the assumption that information transmitted across the corpus callosum is degraded. Indeed, that is one of the two core assumptions of the direct/indirect access theory. No direct test of this critical assumption, however, has ever been reported. The reason for this, as you may suspect, is that no one has ever figured out *how* to measure "signal fidelity" before and after callosal transmission. Nevertheless, despite the fact that the proffered explanation for the enhanced right-field superiority in bilateral presentations rests on this untestable assumption, the phenomenon itself is robust.

As you will recall, we obtained the *very same* difference between bilateral and unilateral presentations in our experiments using *non-linguistic* stimuli, as can be seen in Fig. 40: The right-field detection superiority is markedly enhanced in the circle configuration—where stimuli were present simultaneously in both visual half-fields (a bilateral presentation)—compared to the arc configurations where stimuli were present in only the right or left half-fields (unilateral presentations). An explanation for our results in terms of the concept of hemispheric specialization would require two rather quixotic assumptions: (1) a heretofore undiscovered left hemisphere "vertical stripe detection center" that (2) receives signals of lower "fidelity" from the left visual half-field. Don't laugh—more implausible assumptions than this abound in the laterality literature! The same results, for both words as well as patterns, are much more simply accounted for by a scan having an operating characteristic that tends, across many trials, to examine stimuli in the right visual half-field earlier than those in the left. According to the scanning hypothesis there is indeed a degradation of stimulus information, but it results from the well-established decay of sensory information after a brief stimulus is terminated rather than from a post-hoc assumption that signal fidelity is degraded as a result of callosal transmission.

Decision Time

I have spent sufficient time, I believe, on the differences between the way in which the scanning hypothesis and the hemispheric asymmetry hypothesis account for the right/left performance asymmetries. I now want to tell you a bit more about two other operating characteristics of the scan. The first of these relates to the experiment on the effect of the number of patterns on the target detectability discussed earlier in this chapter (see Figs. 30 and 31). In that experiment the number of non-target patterns in the 12-pattern condition was decreased by deleting them randomly. For terminological convenience, I will define these empty spaces as BLANK stimuli since they represent the absence of a pattern in a location that on many trials did contain a pattern. We found that with more BLANK stimuli overall target detectability increased monotonically, and we concluded that such BLANK stimuli are either not processed at all by the scanning mechanism ("skipped over") or else were processed very quickly, equivalent to the processing of a non-target pattern very easy to discriminate from the target pattern of vertical stripes (Efron, Yund, & Nichols, 1990a). This calls attention to the fact that the non-target patterns we have used are *not* equally difficult to discriminate from the target. For the experiments described so far, however, these differences among the non-target patterns were not relevant to our conclusions since the same *set* of non-target patterns was used for every trial of an experiment.

I now want to describe an experiment (Efron, Yund, & Nichols, 1990c) that tells us how the scanning mechanism deals with *different* types of non-target stimuli. In addition to our usual PATTERNS, we used three other types of stimuli: BLANK, FILL, and DOT stimuli. All four are illustrated in Fig. 41. The FILL stimuli had the same overall luminance as the patterns, but when viewed 4.6° from the fovea they are visually homogeneous, that is, without any internal structure. The DOT stimuli consisted of widely spaced dots, and did have a discernible internal structure when viewed 4.6° from the fovea. The DOT stimuli contain half the number of illuminated pixels as the patterns or the FILL stimuli and thus have half the average luminance.

The non-target PATTERN stimuli, many of which contain vertical spatial frequency components, are most difficult to discriminate from the vertical striped target and therefore would be expected to be processed the slowest. The DOT stimuli, which share some vertical spatial frequencycomponents with the target, would be expected to be processed somewhat faster than the PATTERN stimuli. The FILL stimuli, which do not share any vertical spatial component with the target, would be expected to be

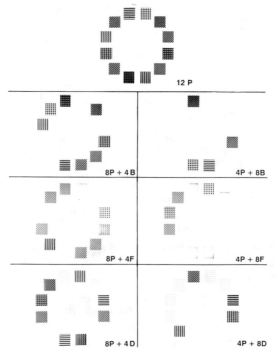

FIGURE 41. Stimuli used by Efron, Yund, and Nichols (1990c). Figure illustrates the seven randomly intermixed conditions described in the text.

processed faster than the DOT stimuli. And, based on our previous experiment, the BLANK stimuli would be expected to be processed the fastest. The assumption underlying these predictions is that it takes the scanner less time to "decide" that a stimulus is *not* the vertical striped target if it does not share features of the target. The greater the number of non-target patterns that can be processed more quickly, the less time it takes for the scan to complete its examination; and the less time that is consumed to complete the scan of the decaying information, the higher will be the overall target detection performance.

Figure 41 illustrates sample trials of the seven randomly intermixed conditions of the experiment. At the top of the figure is the first condition, in which there were 12 patterns (12P). The second condition, on the left below the 12-pattern condition, is a sample trial containing 8 patterns and 4 BLANK stimuli (8P + 4B). Below this is a sample trial containing 8 patterns and 4 FILL stimuli (8P + 4F). The fourth condition, bottom-left, is a trial containing 8 patterns and 4 DOT stimuli (8P + 4D). The fifth condition, illustrated just below and to the right of the 12-pattern condition had 4 patterns and 8 BLANK stimuli (4P + 8B). The sixth condition had 4 patterns and 8 FILL stimuli (4P + 8F), and the seventh condition had 4 patterns and 8 DOT stimuli (4P + 8D). As you can see, the locations of the BLANK, FILL, and DOT stimuli, when present, were distributed randomly among the patterns to counterbalance for any possible effects of configuration or of the particular location of the target within a configuration.

If we assume that it takes the scanner less time to "decide" that a stimulus is not the target if it does not share a feature of the target, then overall target detectability would be expected to increase from the first to the seventh condition. Figure 42 confirms this prediction. The inverse monotonic relationship between target detectability and the number of patterns present is evident by comparing the results of conditions 12P, 8P + 4B and 4P + 8B. This finding, of course, merely confirms what we already knew (see Fig. 31). The inverse relationship also holds for the FILL stimuli, but here it is *less* marked – as expected (compare 12P, 8P + 4F, and 4P + 8F). Finally, for DOT stimuli, which share vertical spatial frequency components with the target, the increase in detectability is the *least* marked (compare 12P, 8P + 4D, and 4P + 8D).

In conclusion, this experiment demonstrates another operating characteristic of the scan. The "decision time" consumed to discriminate each stimulus from the target. In this experiment the decision time is determined by the degree to which each non-target pattern shares spatial frequency components of the target; more generally, it is a direct function of the degree to which each non-target stimulus shares *features* of the target stimulus.

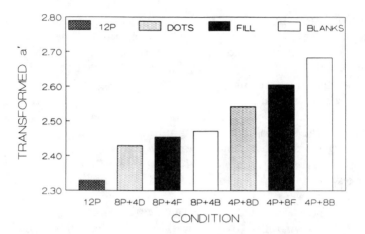

FIGURE 42. Results of experiment illustrated in Fig. 41. The abscissa contains the seven randomly intermixed conditions. The ordinate is the transformed a' measure of target detectability. Reproduced from Efron, Yund, and Nichols (1990c) by permission of *Brain and Cognition* and the authors.

An Attentional or Non-Attentional Scan?

The scanning hypothesis (illustrated numerically in Fig. 33) provides a general description of *any* serial mechanism that is involved in processing short-lived information. It is equally applicable whether the scan is attentional or non-attentional (e.g., perceptual) in nature. I now describe two studies in which we attempted to test the hypothesis that the scan is one of attention. Figure 43 illustrates the first test. The display consists of 24 patterns arranged in three concentric rings of 8 patterns each, centered on the fovea. Using this display we performed two experiments in counterbalanced order on the same group of 80 subjects. In one of these experiments, the subjects were truthfully informed that the target, if present on a trial, would be in any one of the 24 possible locations and that it would be present at all 24 locations with equal probability. In the other experiment, the subjects were truthfully informed that the target, if present on a trial, would *only* be in one of the 8 locations in the *middle ring* of patterns, that it would be present at all 8 possible locations within the ring with equal probability. They were instructed to attend only to these locations and ignore completely the inner and outer rings of patterns. The question, of course, was whether target detectability in the middle ring locations would increase as a result of such selective attention. This did not occur. Not only was the *overall* detectability in the middle ring, collapsed across all 8 locations, virtually the same in the two experiments, but the *shape* of the detectability gradient was also the same. Thus all 24 patterns appear to have been scanned in the *same*

FIGURE 43. Stimuli used by Yund, Efron, and Nichols (1990b). Figure illustrates a 24-pattern experiment, consisting of three concentric "rings" of 8 patterns. Two experiments were performed: In the first, the target was present at every location with equal probability. In the second, the target, if present on a trial was only in the middle ring and the subjects were informed to disregard the inner and outer rings of patterns because the target would never be located there. See text for results. Reproduced by permission of *Brain and Cognition* and the authors.

probabilistic order, despite the fact that the subjects had been instructed to attend selectively to only 8 of them (see Yund, Efron, & Nichols, 1990b for details).

Our second attempt to determine whether the scan is attentional in nature is illustrated in Fig. 44. Three different configurations of 8 patterns were presented in random order. Previous studies by others (Kahneman & Henik, 1977; Neisser, 1963) have provided evidence that the *spatial configuration* of the objects in our visual field is determined by a pre-attentive, perceptual mechanism, and that it is only *after* this initial perceptual processing stage has been completed that attention can be focused on one or another region of the configuration. These previous experiments have shown that items *within* a spatially segregated subgroup are processed at the same time, as reflected by very small and inconsequential differences in detectability or recognition of the items *within* such a spatial subgroup. Yet *large* differences in performance are seen *between* spatially segregated subgroups of items. This has been referred to as the "group processing phenomenon" and is widely considered to be a manifestation of a sequential attentional processing of each of the spatially segregated subgroups.

With respect to the three different configurations of eight patterns seen in Fig. 44, the attentional group processing hypothesis predicts that differences in target detectability *within* a spatially segregated group will be inconsequential, but that large differences in detectability will be observed *between* spatially separated subgroups. For all three configurations illustrated in Fig. 44, however, the experimental results show *marked* differences in detectability among locations *within* a spatially segregated sub-

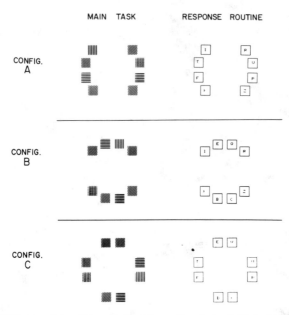

FIGURE 44. Stimuli used by Efron, Yund, and Nichols (1990b). Figure illustrates three randomly intermixed conditions each containing 8 patterns but in three different spatial groupings. On the right side of the figure are the response prompts that appeared following each configuration. The subject was required to indicate the location of the vertically striped target pattern. See text for results. Reproduced by permission of *Brain and Cognition* and the authors.

group, as well as large differences among subgroups: There is *no* evidence of the group processing phenomenon, and thus no evidence that target detection is accomplished by an attentional process (see Efron, Yund, & Nichols, 1990b for details). The point of this experiment, I want to emphasize, is *not* to discredit the idea that the group processing phenomenon, as observed in other experiments, derives from a serial attentional process, but rather to determine whether or not the particular serial processing mechanism we have been studying exhibits this generally accepted characteristic of an attentional process. It doesn't.

The results of the two experiments in Figs. 43 and 44, although failing to provide any evidence that the scan is attentional in nature, do not permit us to reject this possibility. That an attentional scan exists may be taken for granted, but that it is the *only* serial mechanism involved in perceptual information processing is exceedingly unlikely. All one can do, pending the development of a method of measuring attention directly, is to determine if a given serial processing mechanism exhibits the characteristics already identified with an attentional scan.

Scanning Efficiency

In the experiment illustrated in Fig. 44 we observed that *overall* target detectability was *not* the same for the three different spatial configurations of the eight patterns. This finding raised the possibility that the probabilistic order in which the scan examines the stimuli may not be equally *efficient* for all spatial configurations. By efficient, I mean that the *total distance* traversed (the length of the scan path), and thus the time consumed by the scan to complete the examination of all the patterns, may be longer for one spatial configuration than for another. The more specific question to which we wanted an answer was whether or not the scan becomes more efficient with repeated exposures to the *same* configuration. To answer the question we presented only Configuration C of Fig. 44 in three blocks of trials to an inexperienced subject group and analyzed the performance across blocks (Efron, Yund, & Nichols, 1990b).

The results are seen in Fig. 45 where the performance in each block of trials is indicated for positions 1, 3, 4, and 6 in both visual half-fields. Note that for this configuration no pattern or target was ever present at positions 2 and 5. There are two principal findings. The probability of an error in target detection decreases between the first and second block at all

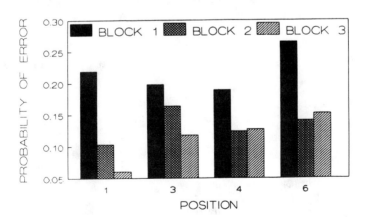

FIGURE 45. Data from Efron, Yund, and Nichols (1990b) using Configuration C of Fig. 44 on every trial. Abscissa contains the four locations from top to bottom of visual field (right and left fields collapsed). Ordinate is the probability of correct response. See text for discussion. Reproduced by permission of *Brain and Cognition* and the authors.

positions, and decreases much less or not at all between the second and third block of trials. This general improvement of performance with practice is not surprising, of course. Nevertheless, it also is evident that scanning efficiency increases as the experiment progresses: The rank order of the error rates at the four positions changes with successive blocks. In the first block of trials the error rates are lowest at positions 3 and 4 and are highest at positions 1 and 6. This implies that initially the scan had a tendency to examine the pair of stimuli near the horizontal meridian first, then went to the top of the field to examine position 1, and then went to the bottom of the field to examine position 6. By the third block of trials, however, the search path changes. It now moves systematically in a downward direction from position 1 to position 6. By the third block of trials, then, the total distance traversed by the scan is appreciably less than in the first block. It becomes more efficient by not "jumping around" so much.

Scanning Consistency

I conclude this summary by describing the intriguing, and wholly unexpected, results of an experiment with illiterate subjects, which provide an unusual insight into a further operating characteristic of the scanning mechanism: scanning consistency. The experiment was performed collaboratively with Professor Ostrosky-Solis at the National University of Mexico, and involved 60 illiterate and 60 literate subjects of the same socioeconomic level (Ostrosky-Solis, Efron & Yund, 1990).

The experiment, illustrated in Fig. 46, employed an arc of 8 patterns all equidistant from the fovea. The subject had to report the location of the vertical striped target that was present on every trial. After the 50 msec exposure to the patterns, boxes containing letters were displayed (illustrated

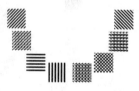

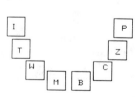

FIGURE 46. Stimuli used by Ostrosky-Solis, Efron, and Yund (1990) in literate and illiterate subjects. The subject was required to point to the location of the vertical stripe target pattern. Reproduced by permission of the authors.

in the lower part of Fig. 46). The illiterate subjects touched the box where they saw the vertical striped target. The literate subjects could either point or call out the appropriate letter. The results are seen in Fig. 47. The locations in each half-field are numbered from upper to lower from 1 to 4 with the letter R or L after the number to indicate the visual half-field. First consider the data at the extreme right of the chart, the two bars denoted by "all." This represents the *overall* detection performance for the literate and illiterate subjects. As you can see, the two groups are virtually *identical* in this respect.

In terms of the numerical model of the scanning hypothesis (Fig. 33) there are three ways this could occur: (1) The two subject groups have identical idealized d' values as well as identical spatial resolution differences among the 8 locations; (2) In one group the decay of information was more rapid but it is *precisely* compensated for by a scan that is more rapid (or by a faster decision time); or (3) In one group the decay of information is less rapid but is *precisely* compensated by a slower scan (or a slower decision time). Of these, the first possibility appears to be the most plausible, and we thus assume that the underlying *physiological* parameters of the scan in the two subject groups are identical.

Next, consider the right- and left-field performance in the two groups. The illiterate subjects have a weak, statistically *non*-significant right-field superiority, the black bar in the RVF is only slightly higher than that in the LVH. The literate subjects, however, have a much more marked right-field

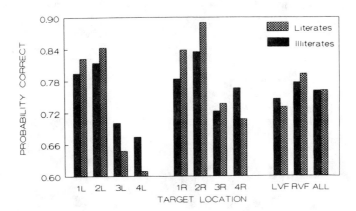

FIGURE 47. Results of experiment illustrated in Fig. 46. The abscissa represents the 8 possible locations for the target. The three pairs of bars on the right of the figure represent the results collapsed within the right (RVF) and left (LVF) visual fields and for both fields together (All). The ordinate is the probability of a correct response. See text for discussion.

superiority, which is statistically significant. The performance of literates in the right field is *better* than that of the illiterates, whereas their performance in the left field is *worse,* a perfect reciprocity relationship.

The remaining data in Fig. 47 demonstrate the detection performance of the two subject groups at each location in each visual half-field. I direct your attention to a major feature of these results. *Within* each half-field, the literate subjects exhibit more marked detectability differences among the locations than do the illiterates. Nevertheless, the *shape* of the detectability gradients in the two groups is very similar: The correlation coefficient between the two sets of 8 values is 0.95. Thus, despite the fact that the shape of the detectability gradients is essentially the same in the two subject groups, you will see in Fig. 47 that there are *major* differences in detectability at almost all of the locations.

The key question is why the two subject groups are so *similar* both with respect to overall performance and to the shape of the detectability gradient, but yet are so *different* at individual locations. The answer becomes apparent when the identical data are presented again in Fig. 48. In this figure the abscissa is not the target location, but the *rank order* of decreasing detectability. Now you can see more clearly that the decrease of detectability in the course of the probabilistic scan is more marked in literate than in illiterate subjects. Indeed, the slope of the function is *twice* as steep in literates as in illiterates: At the first location scanned, the literate subjects have an appreciably *higher* detectability than illiterates but at the last location scanned, they have an appreciably *lower* detectability than the illiterates — with both groups exhibiting an identical *overall* level of perfor-

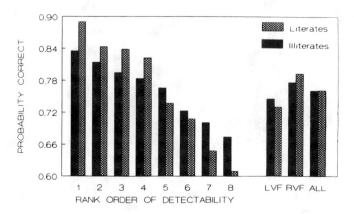

FIGURE 48. Results illustrated in Fig. 47 but replotted on abscissa as rank order of detectability. Note that the slope of the decrease in detectability from the first to the eighth rank order is twice as steep in the literate than in the illiterate subjects. See text for discussion.

mance. This is precisely what the scanning hypothesis predicts will happen if the *only* difference between otherwise identical experiments is a difference of scanning consistency. On that hypothesis the only reason why target detection at locations 1L and 2L is *higher* in literates than in illiterates and that detectability at locations 3L and 4L is *lower* in literates than illiterates, is that the literate subjects are *more consistent* in scanning locations 1L and 2L earlier than locations 3L and 4L (see Fig. 47). The same phenomenon of greater scanning consistency in literate than illiterate subjects is also evident at the same locations in the right half-field.

What are the implications of this conclusion that the literate subjects scan the 8 patterns in a more consistent way than illiterates? Evidently, there is something about reading ability that changes scanning consistency, even for non-linguistic stimuli arranged in a spatial configuration quite unlike that in which text is usually presented. An intriguing possibility is that learning to read *any* language disciplines the scanning mechanism to examine the world in a *orderly* way. I do not mean any particular order — left-to-right in English or right-to-left in Arabic — but rather *more consistently,* in whatever order might be appropriate for the situation.

CONCLUSIONS

And now for a few concluding comments. The primary purpose of this chapter has been to provide a sufficient sampling of our recent work to show how the visual scanning hypothesis might serve as an alternative to the capricious and post-hoc explanations of right/left performance asymmetries in terms of hemispheric specializations. Since the scanning hypothesis contains no inherently asymmetrical assumptions, from a theoretical perspective it is no more concerned with right/left than with upper/lower or any other arbitrarily selected *axis* of the visual field. This chapter focuses on the right-left axis for two reasons. The first, of course, is that it is the *only* axis that has captured the hearts and minds of neuropsychologists. The second is that in the course of our efforts to understand the origin of the complex shape of the detectability gradient, our fundamental goal, we repeatedly found a right/left asymmetrical component of this gradient. True, the *magnitude* of the right/left difference is almost always considerably smaller than the *within-field* differences, as first reported by Heron in 1957. But its ubiquitous presence in all of our experiments obliged us to explore the radically different way in which the scanning hypothesis and the hemispheric specialization hypothesis deal with this phenomenon. In the course of this 6-year exploration we have concluded that many of the phenomena reported in the laterality literature can be more simply accounted for by the existence of a scanning mechanism that examines the contents of the entire visual field and tends to examine some regions in the field earlier than others.

At the present time we know virtually nothing about how this scanning order is determined, except that it is not completely random and that it is influenced by previous visual experience. Any theory that purports to explain how the scanning order is determined, however, will have to be sufficiently general to account for the *entire* detectability gradient, not just one arbitrarily selected axis (right/left or up/down). Needless to say, no dichotomous theory based on hemispheric differences is a particularly promising candidate for such a general explanation.

It is much too early to know how many of the replicable results in the laterality literature can be accounted for by the scanning hypothesis. It will not account for *all* of them. Indeed, one reason for describing experiments with dichotically presented pure tones in Chapter 2 was to show that the asymmetry in pitch processing arises at, or peripheral to, the brain-stem, where frequency information from the two ears is combined. There are undoubtedly *many different* causes of performance asymmetries. Some of them should turn out to be "interesting," in the sense that they lead us to an understanding of more general principles of information processing employed by the brain. Others will probably turn out to be only idiosyncratic phenomena restricted to one or another sensory modality or task and will not contribute to a more general theory.

At some time in the future, the very distant future, some aspect of the right/left *component* of performance asymmetries may prove to be related to the unquestioned anatomical and functional differences between the two cerebral hemispheres. That will not be achieved, however, until some very clever people figure out how to factor out those components of the asymmetry that result from the scanning mechanism. Only then could any *residual* right/left asymmetry be considered to arise from hemispheric differences. Given the description in Chapter 2 of the logical and mathematical requirements that must be fulfilled for such a factor analysis to be successful, I don't anticipate this will be accomplished in the foreseeable future.

My reason for heaping such scorn on the hemispheric specialization hypothesis in Chapters 1 and 2, even to the point of diagnosing a state of brain death, is not that I believe both hemispheres are anatomically and functionally identical. My point is to emphasize that we will never arrive at a correct understanding of the role these hemispheric differences play in cognition if we do not clear up the profound epistemological and conceptual confusions that are proving fatal to the field of laterality research.

The scanning model presented in this Chapter, I submit, represents a viable alternative to the current *post hoc* explanations that typify the prevailing views about performance asymmetries. Whatever the proposed alternative may be, it must be based on explicit assumptions, with testable implications, and must have wide-ranging predictive power. In brief, it must be scientific! I have described only *one* such alternative that meets these minimal requirements. No doubt there will be others in the future.

In preparing this book I had four general goals. The first was to convey how difficult it actually is to infer the function of a part of the brain from the multiple symptoms that result when it is damaged. The second was to show how the phrase "hemispheric specialization" — originally used as a verbal restatement of the fact that lesions in various regions of the brain are correlated with different cognitive deficits — has been erroneously construed as an explanation or hypothesis. This error has caused a major distortion in the interpretation of experimental results and is one of the principal sources for the long list of "specialized" functions currently attributed to each hemisphere. My third goal was to demonstrate that the logical consequences of this error also led to the widespread belief that experiments using dichotic and tachistoscopic presentations in normal subjects would contribute to a deeper understanding of the functional differences between the two hemispheres. You now understand why this optimism can no longer be maintained.

My fourth, and *primary* goal was to increase the probability that, when next you read an article in your morning newspaper or a scientific report that describes yet another hemispheric "specialization," *both* of your cerebral hemispheres will have become appreciably more skeptical. However, should you still believe that it is your *left* hemisphere that is specialized for logical and analytic thought, then I can only offer one bit of friendly advice: If this book ever becomes available on a tape recording, please listen to it again with your *right* ear so that it gets into the appropriate hemisphere!

References

Ardila, A. (1984). Right hemisphere participation in language. In A. Ardila & F. Ostrosky-Solis (Eds.), *The right hemisphere: Neurology and neuropsychology* (pp. 99-107). New York: Gordon and Breach.

Beaumont, J.G. (Ed.). (1982). *Divided visual field studies of cerebral organisation*. London: Academic Press.

Berlin, C.I. (1977). Hemispheric asymmetry in auditory tasks. In S. Harnad, R.W. Doty, L. Goldstein, J. Joyner, & G. Krauthmer (Eds.), *Lateralization in the Nervous System* (pp. 303-323). New York: Academic Press.

Berlin, C., Allen, P., & Parrish, K. (1981). Asymmetries in the binaural interaction of the auditory brainstem response. *Journal of the Acoustical Society of America, 70* (Suppl. S-71).

Berlin, C.I., Lowe-Bell, S.S., Cullen, J.K., Jr., Thompson, C.L., & Stafford, M.R. (1972). Is speech "special"? Perhaps the temporal lobectomy patient can tell us. *Journal of the Acoustical Society of America, 52,* 702-705.

Bertelson, P. (1982). Lateral differences in normal man and lateralization of brain function. *International Journal of Psychology, 17,* 173-210.

Blumstein, S.E., Baker, E., & Goodglass, H. (1977). Phonological factors in auditory comprehension in aphasia. *Neuropsychologia, 15,* 19-30.

Blumstein, S.E., Cooper, W.E., Zurif, E.B., & Caramazza, A. (1977). The perception and production of voice-onset time in aphasia. *Neuropsychologia, 15,* 371-383.

Blumstein, S.E., Goodglass, H., & Tartter, V. (1975). The reliability of ear advantages in dichotic listening. *Brain and Language, 2,* 226-236.

Bopanna, B.B., & Moushegian, G. (1988). Human auditory brainstem asymmetry in the frequency following response (FFR). *Journal of the Acoustical Society of America, 83,* S56.

Bradshaw, J.L., & Nettleton, N.C. (1981). The nature of hemispheric specialization in man. *Behavioral and Brain Sciences, 4,* 51-91.

Broadbent, D.E. (1954). The role of auditory localization in attention and memory span. *Journal of Experimental Psychology, 47,* 191-196.

Bryden, M.P. (1982). *Laterality: Functional asymmetry in the intact brain*. New York:

Academic Press.

Chedru, F., Bastard, V., & Efron, R. (1978). Auditory micropattern discrimination in brain damaged subjects. *Neuropsychologia, 16,* 141-149.

Chiappa, K.H., Gladstone, K.J., & Young, R.R. (1979). Brainstem auditory evoked responses: Studies of waveform variations in 50 normal human subjects. *Archives of Neurology, 36,* 81-87.

Chiarello, C., Dronkers, N.F., & Hardyck, C. (1984). Choosing sides: On the variability of language lateralization in normal subjects. *Neuropsychologia, 22,* 363-373.

Chiarello, C., Knight, R., & Mandel, M. (1982). Aphasia in a prelingually deaf woman. *Brain, 105,* 29-51.

Corballis, M.C. (1983). *Human laterality.* New York: Academic Press.

Curcio, C.A., Sloan, K.R.,Jr., Packer, O., Hendrickson, A.E., & Kalina, R.E. (1987). Distribution of cones in human and monkey retina: Individual variability and radial asymmetry. *Science, 236,* 579-582.

Damasio, H., & Damasio, A.R. (1989). *Lesion analysis in neuropsychology.* Oxford: Oxford University Press.

Decker, T.N., & Howe, S.W. (1981). Auditory tract asymmetry in brainstem electrical responses during binaural stimulation. *Journal of the Acoustical Society of America, 69,* 1084-1090.

Divenyi, P.L., Efron, R., & Yund, E.W. (1977). Ear dominance in dichotic chords and ear superiority in frequency discrimination. *Journal of the Acoustical Society of America, 62,* 624-632.

Divenyi, P.L., & Efron, R. (1979). Spectral vs. temporal features in dichotic listening. *Brain and Language, 7,* 375-386.

Dobie, R.A., & Berlin, C.I. (1979). Binaural interaction in brainstem-evoked responses. *Archives of Otolaryngology, 105,* 391-398

Efron, R. (1963a). The effect of handedness on the perception of simultaneity and temporal order. *Brain, 86,* 261-284.

Efron, R. (1963b). Temporal perception aphasia and déjà vu. *Brain, 86,* 403-424.

Efron, R. (1969). What is perception? In R.S. Cohen & M.W. Wartofsky (Eds.), *Boston studies in philosophy of science* (pp. 137-173). New York: Humanities Press.

Efron, R. (1973). Conservation of temporal information by perceptual systems. *Perception and Psychophysics, 14,* 581-530.

Efron, R., Bogen, J.E., & Yund, E.W. (1977). Perception of dichotic chords by normal and commissurotomized human subjects. *Cortex, 13,* 137-149.

Efron, R., & Crandall, P.H. (1983). Central auditory processing: II. Effects of anterior temporal lobectomy. *Brain and Language, 19,* 237-253.

Efron, R., Crandall, P.H., Koss, B., Divenyi, P.L., & Yund, E.W. (1983). Central auditory processing: III. The 'cocktail party effect' and anterior temporal lobectomy. *Brain and Language, 19,* 254-263.

Efron, R., Koss, B., & Yund, E.W. (1983). Central auditory processing: IV. Ear dominance — Spatial and temporal complexity. *Brain and Language, 19,* 264-282.

Efron, R., Yund, E.W., & Divenyi, P.L. (1979). Individual differences in the perception of dichotic chords. *Journal of the Acoustical Society of America, 66,* 75-86.

Efron, R., Yund, E.W., & Nichols, D.R. (1987). Scanning the visual field without eye movements - A sex difference. *Neuropsychologia, 25,* 637-644.

Efron, R., Yund, E.W., & Nichols, D.R. (1990a). Serial processing of visual spatial patterns in a search paradigm. *Brain and Cognition, 12,* 17-41.

Efron, R., Yund, E.W., & Nichols, D.R. (1990b). Detectability as a function of target location: Effects of spatial configuration. *Brain and Cognition, 12,* 102-116.

Efron, R., Yund, E.W., & Nichols, D.R. (1990c). Visual detectability gradients: The effect of distractors in contralateral field. *Brain and Cognition, 12,* 128-143.

Fairweather, H. (1982). Sex differences. In J. Beaumont (Ed.), *Divided visual field studies of cerebral organization* (pp. 147-194). New York: Academic Press.

Friedman, A., & Polson, M.C. (1981). Hemispheres as independent resource systems: Limited-capacity processing and cerebral specialization. *Journal of Experimental Psychology: Human Perception and Performance, 7,* 1031-1058.

Gazzaniga, M.S. (1983). Right hemisphere language following brain bisection: A 20-year perspective. *American Psychologist, 38, 525-537.*

Gazzaniga, M.S. (1984). Right hemisphere language: Remaining problems. *American Psychologist, 39* (12), 1494-1496.

Gordon, H.W. (1970). Hemispheric asymmetries in the perception of musical chords. *Cortex, 6,* 387-398.

Gregory, A.H. (1982). Ear dominance for pitch. *Neuropsychologia, 20,* 89-90.

Halperin, Y., Nachshon, I., & Carmon, A. (1973). Shift of ear superiority in dichotic listening to temporally patterned nonverbal stimuli. *Journal of the Acoustical Society of America, 53,* 46-50.

Hellige, J.B. (1978). Visual laterality patterns for pure- versus mixed-list presentation. *Journal of Experimental Psychology: Human Perception and Performance, 4,* 121-131.

Hellige, J.B., & Cox, P.J. (1976). Effects of concurrent verbal memory on recognition of stimuli from the left and right visual fields. *Journal of Experimental Psychology: Human Perception and Performance, 2,* 210-221.

Heron, W. (1957). Perception as a function of retinal locus and attention. *American Journal of Psychology, 70,* 38-48.

Hines, D. (1975). Independent functioning of the two cerebral hemispheres for recognizing bilaterally presented tachistoscopic visual-half-field stimuli. *Cortex, 11,* 132-143.

Hines, D. (1976). Recognition of verbs, abstract nouns and concrete nouns from the left and right visual half-fields. *Neuropsychologia, 14,* 211-216.

Hines, D., Fennell, E.B., Bowers, D., & Satz, P. (1980). Left-handers show greater test-retest variability in auditory and visual asymmetry. *Brain and Language, 10,* 208-211.

Hublet, C., Morais, J., & Bertelson, P. (1977). Spatial effects in speech perception in the absence of spatial competition. *Perception, 6,* 461-466.

Julesz, B. (1984). Toward an axiomatic theory of preattentive vision. In G.M. Edelman, W.E. Gall, & W.M. Cowan (Eds.), *Dynamic aspects of neocortical function* (pp. 585-612). New York: Wiley.

Kahneman, D., & Henik, A. (1977). Effects of visual grouping on immediate recall and selective attention. In S. Dornic (Ed.), *Attention and Performance, VI* (pp. 307-332). Hillsdale, NJ: Lawrence Erlbaum Associates.

Kershner, J.R., & Gwan-Rong Jeng, A. (1972). Dual functional hemispheric asymmetry in visual perception: Effects of ocular dominance and postexposural processes. *Neuropsychologia, 10,* 437-445.

Kimura, D. (1961a). Some effects of temporal-lobe damage on auditory perception. *Canadian Journal of Psychology, 15,* 156-165.

Kimura, D. (1961b). Cerebral dominance and the perception of verbal stimuli. *Canadian Journal of Psychology, 15,* 166-171.

Kimura, D. (1964). Left-right differences in the perception of melodies. *Quarterly Journal of Experimental Psychology, 14,* 355-358.

Kimura, D. (1967). Functional asymmetry of the brain in dichotic listening. *Cortex, 3,* 163-178.

Kimura, D., & Folb, S. (1968). Neural processing of backwards-speech sounds. *Science, 161,* 395-396.

Klemm, O. (1925). Ueber die Wirksamkeit kleinster Zeitunterschiede [On the effect of the smallest time differences]. *Archiv gesammter Psychologie, 50,* 204.

Lackner, J.R., & Teuber, H.L. (1973). Alterations in auditory fusion thresholds after cerebral injury in man. *Neuropsychologia, 11,* 409-415.

Lauter, J. (1982). Dichotic identification of complex sounds: Absolute and relative ear advantage. *Journal of the Acoustical Society of America, 71,* 701-707.

McKeever, W.F. (1971). Lateral word recognition: Effects of unilateral and bilateral presentation, asynchrony of bilateral presentation, and forced order of report. *Quarterly Journal of Experimental Psychology, 23,* 410-416.

McKeever, W.F., & Huling, M.D. (1971). Lateral dominance in tachistoscopic word recognition performances obtained with simultaneous bilateral input. *Neuropsychologia, 9,* 15-20.

McNicol, D. (1972). *A primer of signal detection theory.* London: George Allen & Unwin, Ltd.

Milner, B., Taylor, L., & Sperry, R.W. (1968). Lateralized suppression of dichotically presented digits after commissural section in man. *Science, 161,* 184-186.

Mishkin, M., & Forgays, D.G. (1952). Word recognition as a function of retinal locus. *Journal of Experimental Psychology, 43,* 43-48.

Morais, J. (1978). Spatial constraints on attention to speech. In J. Requin (Ed.), *Attention and Performance, VII* (pp. 245-260). Hillsdale, NJ: Lawrence Erlbaum Associates.

Myers, J.J. (1984). Right hemisphere language: Science or fiction? *American Psychologist, 39* (3), 315-320.

Neisser, U. (1963). Decision-time without reaction-time: Experiments in visual scanning. *American Journal of Psychology, 76,* 376-385.

Ojemann, G.A., Fedio, P., & Van Buren, J.M. (1968). Anomia from pulvinar and subcortical parietal stimulation. *Brain, 91,* 99-117.

Ojemann, G.A., & Ward, A.A., Jr. (1971). Speech representation in the ventrolateral thalamus. *Brain, 94,* 669–680.

Orbach, J. (1953). Retinal locus as a factor in recognition of visually perceived words. *American Journal of Psychology, 65,* 555-562.

Ostrosky-Solis, F., Efron, R., & Yund, E.W. (1990). *Visual detectability gradients: Effect of illiteracy.* Manuscript submitted for publication.

Papçun, G., Krashen, S., Terbeek, D., Remington, R., & Harshman, R. (1974). Is the left hemisphere specialized for speech, language and/or something else? *Journal of the Acoustical Society of America, 55,* 319-327.

Poppelreuter, W. (1917). *Die psychischen schadigungen durch Kopfschuss in Kriege 1914-1915* [Physical injuries by gunshot headwounds in the war of 1914-1915]. Leipzig: Voss.

Rijsdijk, J.P., Kroon, J.N., & van der Wildt, G.J. (1980). Contrast sensitivity as a function of position on the retina. *Vision Research, 20,* 235-241.

Robertson, L.C., & Lamb, M. (1988). The role of perceptual reference frames in visual field asymmetries. *Neuropsychologia, 26,* 145-152.

Robertson, L.C., & Lamb, M. (1989). Judging the reflection of misoriented patterns in the right and left visual fields. *Neuropsychologia, 27,* 1081- 1089.

Rosenzweig, M.R. (1951). Representations of the two ears at the auditory cortex. *American Journal of Physiology, 167,* 147-158.

Ross, E.D. (1981). The aprosodias: Functional-anatomic organization of the affective components of language in the right hemisphere. *Archives of Neurology, 38,* 561-569.

Ross, E.D., & Mesulam, M.M. (1979). Dominant language functions of the right hemisphere? Prosody and emotional gesturing. *Archives of Neurology, 36,* 144-148.

Sasanuma, S., Tatsumi, I.F., Kiritani, S., & Fujisaki, H. (1973). Auditory perception of signal duration in aphasia patients. *Annual Bulletin Research of the Institute for Logopedics and Phoniatrics University of Tokyo, 7,* 65-72.

Sparks, R., & Geschwind, N. (1968). Dichotic listening in man after section of neocortical commissures. *Cortex, 4,* 3-16.

Speaks, C., Niccum, N., & Carney, E. (1982). Statistical properties of responses to dichotic listening with CV nonsense syllables. *Journal of the Acoustical Society of America, 72,* 1185-1194.

Springer, S.P., Sidtis, J., Wilson, D., & Gazzaniga, M.S. (1978). Left ear performance in dichotic listening following commissurotomy. *Neuropsychologia, 16,* 305-312.

Swisher, L., & Hirsh, I.J. (1972). Brain damage and the ordering of two temporally successive stimuli. *Neuropsychologia, 10,* 137-152.

Tallal, P., & Newcombe, F. (1978). Impairment of auditory perception and language comprehension in dysphasia. *Brain and Language, 5,* 13-24.

TenHouten, W.D. (1985). Cerebral lateralization theory and the sociology of knowledge. In F. Benson & E. Zaidel (Eds.), *The dual brain* (pp. 341-358). New York: Guilford Press.

Tunturi, A.R. (1946). A study on the pathway from the medial geniculate body to the acoustic cortex in the dog. *American Journal of Physiology, 147,* 311-319.

Vanderplas, J.M., & Garvin, E.A. (1959). The association value of random shapes. *Journal of Experimental Psychology, 57,* 147-154.

Wada, J.A., & Rasmussen, T. (1960). Intracarotid injection of sodium amytal for the lateralization of cerebral speech dominance. *Journal of Neurosurgery, 17,* 266-282.

Walsh, K.W. (1978). *Neuropsychology: A clinical approach.* New York: Churchill Livingstone.

Walshe, F.M.R. (1947). On the role of the pyramidal system in willed movements. *Brain, 70,* 329-354.

Wexler, E., Halwes, T., & Heninger, G.R. (1981). Use of a statistical significance criterion in drawing inferences about hemispheric dominance for language function from dichotic listening data. *Brain and Language, 13,* 13-18.

White, M.J. (1969). Laterality differences in perception: A review. *Psychological Bulletin, 72,* 387-405.

White, M.J. (1973). Does cerebral dominance offer a sufficient explanation for laterality differences in tachistoscopic recognition? *Perceptual and Motor Skills, 36,* 479-485.

Yund, E.W., & Efron, R. (1974). Dichoptic and dichotic micropattern discrimination. *Perception and Psychophysics, 15,* 383-390.

Yund, E.W., & Efron, R. (1977). A model for the relative salience of the pitch of pure tones presented dichotically. *Journal of the Acoustical Society of America, 62,* 607-617.

Yund, E.W., Efron, R., & Divenyi, P.L. (1979). The effect of bone conduction on the intensity independence of dichotic chords. *Journal of the Acoustical Society of America, 65,* 259-261.

Yund, E.W., Efron, R., & Nichols, D.R. (1990a). Detectability gradients as a function of target location. *Brain and Cognition, 12,* 1-16.

Yund, E.W., Efron, R., & Nichols, D.R. (1990b). Detectability as a function of spatial location: Effects of selective attention. *Brain and Cognition, 12,* 42-54.

Yund, E.W., Efron, R., & Nichols, D.R. (1990c). Target detection in one visual field in the presence or absence of stimuli in the contralateral field by right- and left-handed subjects. *Brain and Cognition, 12,* 117-127.

Yund, E.W., Simon, H.J., & Efron, R. (1987). Speech discrimination with an 8- channel compression hearing aid and conventional aids in background of speech-band noise. *Journal of Rehabilitation Research and Development, 24,* 161-180.

Zaidel, E. (1985). Language in the right hemisphere. In F. Benson & E. Zaidel (Eds.), *The dual brain* (pp. 205-231). New York: Guilford Press.

Author Index

Subject Index

A

Agnosia, *see* Visual agnosia
Aphasia, 9–10
  lesions in left hemisphere, 9
  lesions in right hemisphere, 9–10
  lesions in somasthetic cortex, 10
  lesions in thalamus, 10
Asymmetries, 1–3, 9–11, 18–20
  anatomical, 9, 23–25, 102
  electrophysiological, 38–39
  performance, *see* Auditory system, *see* Visual system
Auditory system, 22–26, 30–47, 83
  detectability gradients in, 83
  dichotic listening defined, 22
    melodic stimuli in, 24, 26
    Morse code in, 31
    musical chords in, 26
    pure tone stimuli in, 32–38
    reciprocity relationship in, *see* Reciprocity relationship
    speech sounds in, 22–32, 43–47
    speech-like sounds in, 31, 43–47
    temporal aspects of, 31–32, 46–47
    time-reversed speech in, 31
  ipsilateral suppression in, 23–24, 39–46
    normal subjects and, 23–24
    split-brain subjects and, 38–47

performance asymmetries in, 22–47
  factors affecting, 48, 52–54
  hemispheric specialization inferred from, 24–26, 29–47
  individual differences in, 30
  test-retest reliability in, 30

C

Cerebral laterality and sex, 60–61
Cognitive dysfunction, 5–9, 11–16, 20
  localization *vs* specialization of, 7–11
  reducing multiple deficits to single dysfunction, 11–16
  inherent problems of, 15–16

D

Direct/indirect access theory, 22–25, *see* Kimura, D.
  assumptions of, 23
  impact of, 25–27
  non-refutability of, 27
  resemblance to Ptolemaic theory, 26–27

E

Ear dominance for pitch, *see* Auditory system, pure tone stimuli